For current pricing information,
or to learn more about this or any Nextext title,
call us toll-free at **1-800-323-5435**
or visit our web site at www.nextext.com.

STORIES IN HISTORY

FORGING A
NEW NATION

1765–1790

nextext

Cover illustration: Todd Leonardo

Printed in the United States of America

ISBN 0-618-22209-X

1 2 3 4 5 6 7 — QKT — 08 07 06 05 04 03 02

Table of Contents

PART I: THE ROAD TO REVOLUTION

1765
Patrick Henry Protests the Stamp Act
by Danny Miller

A colonial journalist describes a memorable day in the Virginia House of Burgesses. He tells what happened when fiery speaker Patrick Henry of Virginia attacked the Stamp Act and was accused of treason.

1767
The Daughters of Liberty Stage a Boycott
by Judith Lloyd Yero

The English government continued to find ways to tax the American colonists. In this story, a Massachusetts woman tells how her friend Mercy Otis Warren urged American women to refuse to buy British goods.

PART II: THE REVOLUTIONARY WAR

PART III: FROM CONFEDERATION TO CONSTITUTION

In the mid-1780s in Massachusetts, farmers deeply in debt were worried about losing their farms. Even worse, the courts were sending men to prison for not paying their debts. In this story, farm families try to decide whether to join Daniel Shays in an armed rebellion against the courts.

A delegate to the Constitutional Convention describes the debate over the issue of states' rights. Who should have more power—the states or the national government?

About this Book

The stories are historical fiction. They are based on historical fact, but some of the characters and events may be fictional. In the Sources section, you'll learn which is which, and where the information came from.

The illustrations are all historical. If they are from a time different from the story, the caption tells you. Original documents help you understand the time period. Maps let you know where things were.

Items explained in People and Terms to Know are repeated in the Glossary. Look there if you come across a name or term you don't know.

Historians do not always know or agree on the exact dates of events in the past. The letter c before a date means "about" (from the Latin word circa).

If you would like to read more about these exciting times, you will find recommendations in Reading on Your Own.

Background

"We hold these truths to be self-evident,
that all men are created equal . . ."

—Declaration of Independence, 1776

▲

Paul Revere rides to warn a farmer, "The British are coming!"

The Road to Revolution

"Taxation without representation is tyranny!"

—James Otis, c. 1761

Conflict between Great Britain and the thirteen colonies did not develop overnight. In fact, things were generally good from the time Jamestown was settled in 1607 until the French and Indian War (1754–1763). It was what happened after this war that caused things to change for the worse.

Great Britain Taxed the Colonies

In the French and Indian War, the British tried to drive the French out of North America. The colonists did their part to help. They thought of themselves as loyal British subjects. The British would not have been able to defeat the French without the help of the colonists.

Everything changed with the war's end. After nine years of fighting, Great Britain was very much in debt. To help pay for the costs of the war, Parliament—Great Britain's lawmaking body—decided to increase taxes in the colonies.

A tax on sugar brought some mild protests from the colonies. But the Stamp Act that followed was a different story. The Stamp Act required colonists to buy stamps and place them on all legal documents. They even had to buy stamps for items such as newspapers, pamphlets, and playing cards.

Next came the Declaratory Act, in which Parliament said that it could lay any tax it wanted to on the colonies. A final blow to the colonists came in 1767 with the passage of the Townshend Acts. These laws placed taxes on tea, paper, glass, lead, and paint.

The Colonies Protested

To the colonists, the Stamp Act was a clear case of "taxation without representation." Men in different colonies began to form secret protest groups called the Sons of Liberty. These groups attacked British stamp sellers and burned bundles of stamps. Then colonists decided to refuse to buy British goods. That got the attention of Parliament. After a few months, British merchants began to lose money, and Parliament cancelled the act.

The Boston Massacre

Colonial unrest grew. More British troops were sent to the colonies to keep control. Violence was bound to break out. On March 5, 1770, a group of British soldiers fired into a Boston mob. Five people were killed and several others were wounded. Although the soldiers fired in self-defense, word spread that they were ordered to shoot. The event aroused hatred of the British.

The Boston Tea Party

In England, too, some leaders felt the Americans were not being treated fairly. The British government did away with the taxes on everything except tea. Anger eased, but anti-British feelings did not die. Then, in 1773, some members of the Sons of Liberty dressed as Indians and boarded several British ships in Boston Harbor. They dumped more than 340 chests of tea into the water. Many townspeople secretly supported this act.

British reaction to the Boston Tea Party was swift. Parliament passed laws that came to be called the Intolerable Acts. *Intolerable* means unbearable, or not acceptable. One law closed the port of Boston. Another, called the Quartering Act, said the colonists had to house British troops in their private homes. These acts angered colonists everywhere and led to the meeting of the First Continental Congress in September 1774. At this meeting, colonial leaders debated ways to get the British government to give colonists back their rights. Seven months later, the Revolutionary War began.

▲

This famous political cartoon reminds the colonists of the danger of not sticking together.

The Revolution Began

The opening shots of the American Revolution were fired at Lexington, Massachusetts, on April 19, 1775. A British force on its way to Concord to seize a store of colonial weapons clashed with about 70 colonial volunteer soldiers. No one knows for sure who fired first, but "the shot heard round the world" left eight Americans dead.

The British marched on to Concord, where they were met by a larger group of Americans. After a brief fight, the British turned and headed back to Boston. Along the way, American riflemen shot at them from behind trees and fences. More than 250 British soldiers were killed or wounded.

After Lexington and Concord, a Second
Continental Congress met and set up the
Continental Army. George Washington was put in
charge of the troops.

The first real battle of the war took place on a
hill above Boston. The battle has always been
known as the Battle of Bunker Hill. But, in truth, the
battle was fought on nearby Breed's Hill. American
forces had taken a position on the hill, and the
British were determined to drive them from it. Two
British charges were turned back, and the British
suffered great losses. After the third charge, the
Americans ran out of ammunition. They were
forced to retreat from the hill.

The Battle of Bunker Hill (June 17, 1775) was
not an American victory, but it boosted the spirits
of the American troops. It proved that they could
hold their own against British regulars, the finest
soldiers in the world.

Common Sense and the Declaration
of Independence

Seven months after the Battle of Bunker Hill, a
pamphlet of great importance appeared in the
colonies. It was titled *Common Sense* and was
written by Thomas Paine. Paine called on the

colonists to break with England and set up an independent nation.

Even after fighting had gone on for seven months, most Americans hoped to reach an agreement with England. Thomas Paine's pamphlet changed all that. In *Common Sense*, he pointed out

▲
A cheering crowd hears of the signing of the Declaration of Independence.

Early Battles of the Revolution

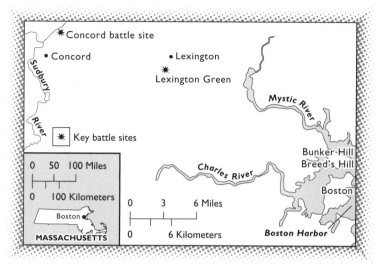

reasons why the time had come to part with the mother country.

Six months after *Common Sense* appeared, the Declaration of Independence was signed in Philadelphia. After that, there was no turning back. The colonies were now committed to cooperate and fight. If their struggle failed, they faced serious punishment. Benjamin Franklin was one of the signers of the Declaration of Independence. Perhaps he put it best when he said: "We must indeed all hang together, or, most assuredly, we shall all hang separately."

The Revolutionary War

"I know not what course others may take, but as for me, give me liberty or give me death!"

—Patrick Henry, in a speech before the Virginia House of Burgesses (legislature), March 23, 1775

Patriots and Loyalists

When war broke out, a third of the people in the colonies favored separation from Great Britain. They were called *Patriots*. Another third announced their loyalty to the Crown. They were called *Loyalists*. Both groups disliked the final third, which tried to stay neutral.

During the Revolutionary War, about 220,000 men served in the Continental Army. But this number is misleading. General George Washington, as commander in chief, rarely had more than 20,000 troops available at any given time.

About 50,000 Loyalists fought alongside Great Britain's more than 40,000 soldiers. The British troops included about 30,000 soldiers for hire. Because many of these hired soldiers came from the German state of Hesse, they were all known as *Hessians*.

C.W. Peale painted this ▶
portrait of Washington
at Princeton in 1779.

The Continental Army was created in June 1775. Throughout the war, the army never had enough food, supplies, equipment, ammunition, or transport. In addition, there were never enough soldiers. Soldiers were paid very little, so they signed up for only short periods of time. When their time was up, the men wanted to go home to take care of their farms and families. Outbreaks of typhus and smallpox also took a great toll on the numbers. Still, General Washington, the commander of the Continental Army, kept his forces together and led them to victory in 1781.

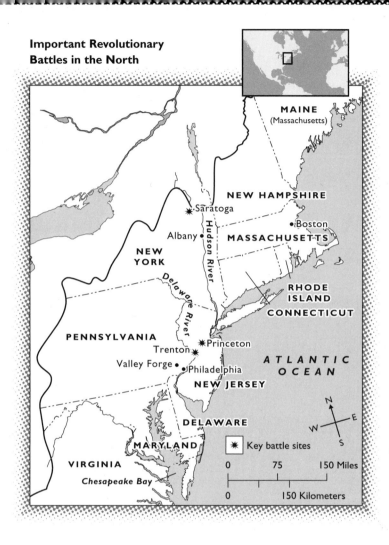

Important Revolutionary Battles in the North

MAINE (Massachusetts)

NEW HAMPSHIRE

Saratoga

Albany • Boston

MASSACHUSETTS

NEW YORK

Hudson River

Delaware River

RHODE ISLAND

CONNECTICUT

PENNSYLVANIA

Princeton

Trenton

Valley Forge • Philadelphia

ATLANTIC OCEAN

NEW JERSEY

DELAWARE

✳ Key battle sites

MARYLAND

0   75   150 Miles

VIRGINIA

Chesapeake Bay

0   150 Kilometers

N

W — E

S

Washington was without doubt the most important leader on the American side. People loved him for his courage. He once remarked that there was something "charming" in the whistle of bullets during battle. His popularity helped unite the Americans.

War in the North

Despite early setbacks in New York, General Washington won several important victories in New Jersey. On Christmas night in 1776, he completely surprised a force of Hessians camped at Trenton. He captured more than 900 of the enemy and seized 6 cannons and 1,000 muskets.

One week later, Washington surprised and defeated a British force at nearby Princeton. His two victories in New Jersey helped to raise American spirits.

Nine months after Trenton and Princeton, the war turned in the Patriots' favor. In October 1777 an American army led by General Horatio Gates defeated General John Burgoyne's British and Hessian force at Saratoga, New York. Gates's victory proved to be the turning point of the war.

War in the South

Sometime in 1778, the war shifted to the South. (See map on page 129.) In 1780, the British captured Savannah, Georgia, and Charleston, South Carolina. When they followed this up with a victory at Camden, South Carolina, things looked bad for the Patriots.

After Camden, however, American fortunes began to change. Under Francis Marion, guerrilla fighters (those who hit and run) kept the British off balance. Marion became known as the "Swamp Fox" because, after striking at the British, he would retreat into the swamplands of the Carolinas. He and others drew the British into Virginia. Finally, the British commander Charles Cornwallis found himself trapped in Virginia. Cornwallis was defeated at Yorktown in 1781. His surrender ended the war.

Help from Europe

After General Gates's victory at the Battle of Saratoga, France entered the war against Great Britain. But even before France got involved, there were individuals in Europe who agreed with the Patriot cause and offered their help.

One of the first was the Marquis de Lafayette from France. He served as a major general in Washington's army when he was only 19 years old. Another was Thaddeus Kosciuszko from Poland, who was a colonel of engineers during the war. Then there was the German general Baron Johann De Kalb, who fought bravely with the Americans in the South. And there was Baron Friedrich Wilhelm von Steuben, also from Germany. He was an excellent drill master. His efforts helped turn Washington's army into an effective fighting force during the terrible winter at Valley Forge in 1777–1778.

The Home Front

Americans on the home front pitched in, too. Women took care of farms and businesses in their husbands' absence. They also rolled bandages, made clothes for soldiers, cared for the wounded, and helped make gunpowder and cannonballs. Some served as spies, and a few even fought as soldiers.

Children also did their part. They took on extra duties at home and helped make supplies for the troops. Some who were older served as guides and unofficial spies. Their efforts were heroic, considering that they were almost always hungry. Food at home was scarce, and so were many everyday supplies.

▲
Nancy Hart defends her home against the British.

From Confederation to Constitution

"If men were angels, no government would be necessary."

—James Madison
The Federalist, Number 51

The Articles of Confederation

When the colonies declared independence, Great Britain no longer ruled them. A government was needed, and the colonial leaders agreed to work together. They drew up a plan that they called the Articles of Confederation.

There were two reasons why the former colonists formed a confederation that gave little authority to the national government. First, each of the former colonies wanted to keep its independence. Second, after years of British rule, colonists feared a government with too much power.

Even though the national government was weak under the Articles, it did score several successes. It won the war with Great Britain and worked out peace terms. It also set up rules for governing the Northwest Territory. The Northwest

In 1787, delegates gathered at the Pennsylvania State House. ▶

Territory was the vast area of land between the Great Lakes and the Ohio and Mississippi rivers.

But the Articles of Confederation had many more weaknesses than strengths. It did not provide for an executive branch or national courts. It did not give Congress the power to tax or control trade. In addition, each state had its own money and army. Confusion ruled. Under such conditions, it is easy to see why changes were needed.

The Constitutional Convention

In May 1787, delegates from every state except Rhode Island met in Philadelphia to change the Articles of Confederation. In the end, however, they wrote a new plan of government. That new plan was the Constitution.

Many important men attended the convention. They included George Washington, Benjamin Franklin, and Alexander Hamilton. One, James Madison, did most of the actual writing of the new plan. For this reason, he is often called the "Father of the Constitution."

The Fight and Ratification

The main issue debated at the Constitutional Convention had to do with representation in

Congress. The large states felt they should have more representatives. The smaller states felt that each state should have the same number. A compromise, or agreement, was made, creating the two houses of Congress as they exist today. Each state has two senators in the Senate, while representation in the House is based on population.

Once adopted, the Constitution had to be ratified (approved) by nine of the thirteen states. The first state to ratify was Delaware. The ninth was New Hampshire. The new government went into effect on March 4, 1789.

The U.S. Constitution is a work of genius. It lays the foundation for a government that balances people's rights with their need for government. Never before had such ideas been so well spelled out. Never before had a system of checks and balances protected people from too much power in their government. The Constitution is the oldest document of its kind. Many other nations' constitutions have been modeled after it.

Time Line

1765—Stamp Act is passed.

1767—Townshend Acts are passed.

1770—Boston Massacre takes place.

1773—Boston Tea Party takes place.

1774—Intolerable Acts passed; First Continental Congress meets.

1775—Battles fought at Lexington, Concord, and Bunker Hill.

1776—*Common Sense* is published; Declaration of Independence is signed.

1777—Americans defeat British at Saratoga; Americans suffer great hardship during winter at Valley Forge.

1778—France enters war on American side.

1779—John Paul Jones wins naval victory over *Serapis*.

1781—British surrender at Yorktown; last state ratifies Articles of Confederation

1783—Treaty of Paris signed.

1787—Northwest Ordinance passed; Shays's Rebellion takes place; Constitutional Convention meets.

1789—George Washington becomes first U.S. president.

1790—Last state ratifies the Constitution.

1791—Bill of Rights ratified.

The Road to Revolution

Patrick Henry Protests the Stamp Act

BY DANNY MILLER

Thomas Washburn ran all the way home from the explosive session at Virginia's **House of Burgesses**.

"Sarah!" he shouted, trying to catch his breath as he entered the doorway of their **Williamsburg** home. It was May 29, 1765. Thomas was a reporter for the *Virginia Gazette* and had spent many long hours covering the events at the House of Burgesses, but he had never seen anything like this.

Sarah Washburn met her husband at the door. With her was her brother, Oliver Hailey. Oliver was visiting Williamsburg after spending six months living on the **western frontier**.

People and Terms to Know

House of Burgesses—law-making branch of colonial Virginia's government.

Williamsburg—capital of colonial Virginia.

western frontier—western border. At the time of the story (1765) it was the Ohio River Valley.

Bostonians protested the Stamp Act by burning stamped paper.

"What is it, Thomas?" Sarah asked, helping her husband take off his wool jacket.

"**Treason**!" he panted, still out of breath. "They accused **Patrick Henry** of treason!"

"Patrick Henry!" Sarah exclaimed, "the **Patriot** who just joined the House of Burgesses less than two weeks ago! What on earth happened, Thomas?"

"Oh, it was quite a scene! This morning Henry presented a series of powerful arguments against the **Stamp Act**."

"What is the Stamp Act?" Oliver asked. News was hard to come by on the frontier, and Oliver was not up-to-date on the activities of the colonies.

"It's the tax law that was passed by **Parliament** earlier this year. It's supposed to go into effect on November 1, but plenty of people are against it.

"It means that we will have to buy a special stamp for nearly every piece of printed paper we use,"

People and Terms to Know

Treason—high crime of betrayal of or disloyalty to one's country.

Patrick Henry—(1736–1799) American lawyer, Patriot, and public speaker.

Patriot—member of the group of colonists who thought the colonies should be a country independent from Britain. Only about one-third of all colonists were Patriots.

Stamp Act—law passed by the British Parliament in March 1765 requiring American colonists to buy a tax stamp for all printed materials.

Parliament—legislative (law making) branch of government in Great Britain. It includes the House of Lords and the House of Commons.

explained Sarah. "That includes newspapers, licenses, diplomas, even playing cards!"

"It's unbelievable!" said Oliver. "First they gave us the **Navigation Acts**, and now this!"

"At least those laws were about controlling trade. I can almost understand that. But the Stamp Act is different— it's just a tax. Its only purpose is to raise money for Great Britain.

"Its only purpose is to raise money for Great Britain."

"The British government claims that the extra taxes are needed to pay for the troops that they keep in America," Sarah continued, "especially after the recent **Indian Wars**."

Thomas sat down on one of the wooden chairs in their small living room and started pulling off his heavy leather boots. "One House member told me yesterday that it isn't even the money that bothers

---

People and Terms to Know

Navigation Acts—series of laws passed by Parliament to control trade between England and its colonies.

Indian Wars—French and Indian War (1754–1763), in which American colonists and British soldiers battled the French and their Indian allies over which European power would control most of North America.

him so much. It's the standard this new tax sets. If we accept this law without protest, what other heavy taxes will we be expected to pay in the future?"

"I trust the colonists have risen up against the unfair legislation?" Oliver asked, feeling slightly embarrassed that he was no longer well informed about current events in the colonies.

"Yes," Thomas said, "and the good news is that the protests have united us colonists more closely than ever before. But most of the protests have fallen on deaf ears. In London, **Benjamin Franklin** pleaded for the **repeal** of the Stamp Act, but he wasn't successful. When I interviewed him after he got back, he told me that the tide was too strong against us and that we'd have better luck stopping the sun from setting!"

Sarah had kept up with all the protests in Virginia and the neighboring colonies. "Nearly all of the colonies sent **petitions** protesting the act," she said. "But now many people seem to have

---

People and Terms to Know

Benjamin Franklin—(1706–1790) American statesman, author, and scientist.
repeal—cancel officially; undo.
petitions—formal requests for rights or benefits from an authority.

given up the fight. They think the Stamp Act will be put into effect later this year."

"It's true," said Thomas. "I didn't hear any protests when the House of Burgesses met earlier this month. One member told me that they were still very much against the tax. They just didn't see what more they could do about it."

"Ah," Oliver said, "but that was before Patrick Henry entered the picture, right, Thomas?"

"Yes, our newest **burgess** has certainly brought new blood to the fight. Oh, Sarah and Oliver, I wish you could have heard this man speak today!"

"I heard that he is quite young," said Sarah, spooning some bean porridge into a bowl from a big iron pot in the fireplace. "Is that true?"

"As a matter of fact, today is the man's twenty-ninth birthday. But he seems much older. Did you know that Henry is an expert in colonial law? He based his arguments against the Stamp Tax on the earliest treaties between England and the colonies."

Sarah placed the bowl of porridge in front of her husband. She was eager to hear more about the events of the day.

People and Terms to Know

burgess—member of Virginia's colonial legislature.

"Henry read a series of resolutions, or statements, that he had written on a blank sheet of paper torn from a law book. He claimed that, by law, Americans have the same rights as the English. Those rights, he said, include the right to be taxed only by our own representatives. In his fifth resolution, he claimed that only the General Assembly of this colony has the right to tax the people who live here. He said that any attempt by others to tax us will destroy British as well as American freedom!"

"He said that any attempt by others to tax us will destroy British as well as American freedom!"

"I can imagine how some of the burgesses reacted to those words," Sarah said. "They probably thought it was a direct threat to the King!"

"You guessed it," Thomas said. "That's when Speaker Robinson and a group of others cried 'Treason!' causing the whole place to erupt into a shouting match."

"How did Henry respond?" Oliver asked.

"He just stood there. He didn't back down. Finally, he shouted back to them, 'If *this* be treason, make the most of it!'"

Patrick Henry.

"We need men like that on the western frontier," said Oliver. "I think Patrick Henry has a fine career ahead of him in politics!"

"Most definitely he does," said Thomas, taking a bite of the cornbread Sarah had placed in his bowl. "You should have seen how he held the attention of the crowd. His voice rose louder and louder until the walls of the building seemed to shake. People were leaning forward in their seats. The room was crowded with townsfolk. And many students from the College of William and Mary stood in the doorway, cheering Henry on. After the speech, one young lawyer named **Thomas Jefferson** said that 'Patrick Henry spoke as **Homer** wrote.'"

"But did Henry's resolutions pass?" Sarah asked.

"There was a wild debate that I thought might turn violent. But in the end, the resolutions did pass by a small majority—maybe just one or two votes!"

"This challenge to England will make some people very angry," Sarah said, suddenly worried about the future.

"No doubt it will," Thomas said. "I already heard that our English governor is so angry about today's events that he's threatening to close down the House of Burgesses!"

"I hope it's the beginning of a time that will bring us real independence once and for all," said Oliver.

"We'll see," Thomas said. "But now I must go write my article so that everyone in the colonies can read about Patrick Henry's brave actions. One thing is for sure—exciting times are ahead of us!"

People and Terms to Know

Thomas Jefferson—(1743–1826) American statesman who became the third president of the United States (1801–1809).

Homer—Greek poet and author of two famous long poems, the *Iliad* and the *Odyssey*, written around 750 B.C.

*   *   *

Patrick Henry's fifth resolution was later repealed. The other four resolutions held. They supported the idea that colonists should enjoy all the rights of British subjects. The House of Burgesses was, in fact, dissolved, or closed down, by the governor of Virginia. The colonists continued to resist the Stamp Act until it was finally repealed by Parliament in March 1766.

QUESTIONS TO CONSIDER

1. Why were many American colonists opposed to the Stamp Act?

2. What is your opinion of the kinds of actions Americans took to protest the Act?

3. Why do you think some members of the House of Burgesses shouted "Treason!" after Patrick Henry's speech?

4. What were Patrick Henry's main arguments against the Stamp Act in his resolutions?

Patrick Henry's Resolutions

In his speech against the Stamp Act on May 29, 1765, Patrick Henry offered the following five resolutions:

That the colonists have the same rights and privileges as citizens of Great Britain.

That two royal charters granted many years earlier by King James I had declared that all colonists have the same liberties as if they had been born in England.

That British citizens can only be taxed by their own representatives.

That the Virginia colony has always been governed by its own Assembly and that this has always been recognized by the kings and people of Great Britain.

That only the Assembly in Virginia has the right to tax the people who live there.

Give Me Liberty: The Story of the Declaration of Independence
by Russell Freedman

Patrick Henry, Paul Revere, and the events leading up to the American Revolution come alive in this exciting account. Primary sources such as newspaper articles, letters, popular verses, and a variety of images further enliven the text.

Annie Henry and the Birth of Liberty
by Susan Olasky

Patrick Henry was known for his exciting speeches, and this book tells how his daughter Annie takes after her father. At the time of the Revolution, though, Annie's high spirits may put her in danger.

Where Was Patrick Henry on the 29th of May?
by Jean Fritz

Patrick Henry was not just a hero of the American Revolution. He was also a planter before he became a politician. Find out how he grew up in Virginia, how he became a statesman, and how he came to be at the front of efforts for independence.

The Daughters of Liberty Stage a Boycott

BY JUDITH LLOYD YERO

Plymouth, Massachusetts
September 2, 1767

My Dear Friend Susannah,

I am sorry I have taken so long to answer your welcome letter. I was very pleased at the news of your coming marriage. The only sad note is that it comes at a time of such unrest. The upsetting events here have kept me from putting pen to paper sooner.

Our joy at the repeal of the evil Stamp Act was short-lived. Our British cousins continue to treat us badly. Their latest attack on our freedom has everyone here up in arms.

People and Terms to Know

In title: **boycott**—refusal of a group to buy or provide goods or services. The word *boycott* was first used in the 1880s, when laborers in County Mayo, Ireland, refused to work for Captain Boycott, the agent of an English landowner.

Mrs. Thomas Mifflin, pictured here with her husband in their home, is spinning thread to make her own clothes so that she will not need to buy

A woman shops for furs. Women gave up such luxuries to support the revolutionary cause.

How dare the Parliament declare that we must pay taxes on lead, glass, paint, paper, silk, linen, and tea? These British products cost us enough now! They ran their treasury dry trying to add to their lands on this continent. Now they want more money from us!

We have no say in the decisions of Parliament, yet they feel free to tax us to pay for their mistakes. Why should we pay the wages of the very men who take our liberties from us?

If I sound unladylike, I beg your understanding. Feelings run high against this latest insult. We women may not take part in political decisions. We may not take up arms in defense of our liberty. But we are not helpless. Already, we have thought of ways to help the cause.

The words of Mr. **Samuel Adams** have fired the spirit of the people. The cry of "No taxation without representation" rings through meeting halls and in the streets. Mr. Adams has declared that "The right to freedom being a gift of God, it is not in the power of man to **alienate** this gift and **voluntarily** become a slave."
I expect that all the colonies will soon join forces against this latest outrage.

I expect that all the colonies will soon join forces against this latest outrage.

Forgive me for going on so. Your own days must be filled with happier thoughts and plans for your wedding. I am most interested in hearing about your future husband and the home you will be building. I trust that these insults the British have heaped upon us will not dampen your joy.

Fondest regards,
Felicia

People and Terms to Know

Samuel Adams—(1722–1803) leader of Boston protests against the British and a signer of the Declaration of Independence.

alienate—set aside.

voluntarily—of one's own free will.

Philadelphia, Pennsylvania

October 4, 1767

Dearest Felicia—

Your letter came at a time when we ourselves were feeling a rush of anger. These latest laws threaten our God-given freedoms. My dear Charles and I have spent many hours talking about how this new threat might affect our future. We have decided to put off our wedding until the times become more peaceful.

I am most interested in how you and the other women plan to aid the cause of freedom. There are many women here who share our love of country. If you will share your thoughts, I will see to it that our efforts will be added to your own. I eagerly await your response.

Hopefully,
Susannah

*   *   *

Plymouth, Massachusetts
November 10, 1767

M y Dearest Susannah,

I am unhappy that this unrest has made you change your plans. However, we must defend our freedom. I trust that you and the other women of Philadelphia will join the **Daughters of Liberty** in our noble cause.

We have decided to teach the British a lesson about the resolve of the colonists. One of our most outspoken ladies, **Mercy Otis Warren**, said what all of us feel. She

American poet, historian, and playwright Mercy Otis Warren. ▶

People and Terms to Know

Daughters of Liberty—organization of women who supported the boycott of British goods. Instead of buying items made in England, the women made their own.

Mercy Otis Warren—(1728–1814) writer and poet who, with her brother, James Otis, and her husband, James Warren, took an active role in protests against the British. The Warren home was a meeting place for revolutionaries, including John Adams, who would later be elected president. In 1805, Mercy Warren published a three-volume history of the Revolution.

said she was sure that all of us would rather dress in goatskin than English cloth!

If Parliament is greedy enough to tax us without mercy, then they will get what they deserve.

> *If Parliament is greedy enough to tax us without mercy, then they will get what they deserve.*

We will refuse to buy their goods—not only those that are taxed, but all British goods. We are not so weak that we must have their fancy British cloth for our clothing or their tea for our thirst. They will quickly feel the pinch when our money no longer reaches their pockets.

If you and your friends wish to join our efforts, there are many things you can do. Wear only **homespun** cloth. We gather for **spinning bees** weekly. We spin yarn from the wool of sheep and weave the cloth for all of our needs.

We have organized an Anti-Tea League and refuse to buy or drink the hateful British herb.

People and Terms to Know

homespun—rough cloth made from yarn spun at home. All social classes wore clothing made of homespun cloth during the boycott of British goods.

spinning bees—gatherings at which women spun wool into yarn for making clothing.

Mercy Warren gathers herbs and dries them with her own hands. She brews raspberry leaves, currant, and sage into an agreeable tea. I must admit that these beverages are not as satisfying as the British tea, but the sacrifice is necessary. The drinking of coffee has become more common.

I am sure that you and your friends can think of ways to do without British goods. Our shopkeepers' shelves are overflowing with goods we refuse to touch. They are even now crying to their British suppliers about how the **Townshend Acts** are hurting them. We will keep up this fight until the British are convinced of our purpose. Even if every man in the colonies is defeated, the British will still have to deal with the women!

With highest regard,
Felicia

*　　*　　*

People and Terms to Know

Townshend Acts—(1767) series of British laws putting taxes on such imported products as tea, paint, paper, and glass sold in the American colonies. The Acts were made to replace the income lost when the Stamp Act was repealed.

Philadelphia, Pennsylvania

July 9, 1768

M_y Dear Friend Felicia—

Since my last letter, we have added even more actions to our efforts. One of our ladies has published a poem in the *Pennsylvania Gazette*. You would rejoice at her spirit. In powerful words, she declares that we will decorate our homes with the flowers of the meadow and color our clothing with the juice of berries rather than pay the hateful British taxes on paints and dyes. Humorously, she says that if we run out of paper, we will write on leaves or speak more loudly.

> "Stand firmly resolve'd, and bid **Grenville** to see,
> That rather than freedom we part with our tea,
> And well as we love the dear draught [drink]
>   when a-dry [thirsty],
> As American Patriots our taste we deny."

People and Terms to Know

Grenville—George Grenville (1712–1770), English politician who made the colonists angry by supporting the Stamp Act and the Townshend Acts.

We will win. Our efforts will show those greedy British that the colonists will not submit to their **tyranny**.

As always,
Susannah

*　　*　　*

Plymouth, Massachusetts
April 29, 1770

My Dear Friend, Susannah,

We have won! Reports from London tell of a seven-year **surplus** of tea piling up in the British warehouses. Parliament has given in to the pleas of British merchants to repeal the Townshend Acts. Although there is still a tax on tea, the taxes have been removed from all of the other goods.

We have not ended our protests. We will refuse to buy their tea and continue to protest until we get the representation that our growing nation deserves. Perhaps we do not need the British at all.

People and Terms to Know

tyranny (TIHR•uh•nee)—unchecked power.
surplus—more than is needed; excess.

The colonies have grown into a territory worthy of being its own nation. Only time will tell if we will be forced to that action.

I am overjoyed that you and Charles have finally decided to be married. You have my fondest wishes for a life of happiness and joy.

Yours,
Felicia

QUESTIONS TO CONSIDER

1. What was Samuel Adams talking about when he cried, "No taxation without representation"?

2. What is your opinion of the steps the women of the colonies took to help the men protest the actions of Parliament?

3. What effect did the women's actions have on their own daily lives?

4. Why did Parliament finally repeal the Townshend Acts?

The Daughters of Liberty

This poem appeared in the *Pennsylvania Gazette* in 1768. Most people believe that it was written by an unknown Quaker woman living in Philadelphia. The poem expresses the patriotic feelings that so many people shared at the time.

Since the men, from a party or fear of a frown,
Are kept by a sugar-plum quietly down,
Supinely asleep—and depriv'd of their sight,
Are stripp'd of their freedom, and robb'd of
    their right;
If the sons, so degenerate! the blessings despise,
Let the Daughters of Liberty nobly arise;
And though we've no voice but a negative here,
The use of the taxables, let us forbear:—
(Then merchants import till your stores are
    all full,
May the buyers be few, and your traffic be dull!)

Stand firmly resolv'd, and bid Grenville to see,
That rather than freedom we part with our tea,
And well as we love the dear draught when
    a-dry,

As American Patriots our taste we deny—
Pennsylvania's gay meadows can richly afford
To pamper our fancy or furnish our board;
And paper sufficient at home still we have,
To assure the wiseacre, we will not sign slave;
When this homespun shall fail, to remonstrate
    our grief,
We can speak viva voce, or scratch on a leaf;
Refuse all their colors, though richest of dye,
When the juice of a berry our paint can supply,
To humor our fancy—and as for our houses,
They'll do without painting as well as our
    spouses;
While to keep out the cold of a keen winter morn,
We can screen the north-west with a well pol-
    ished horn;
And trust me a woman, by honest invention,
Might give this state-doctor a dose of prevention.

Join mutual in this—and but small as it seems,
We may jostle a Grenville, and puzzle his
    schemes;
But a motive more worthy our patriot pen,
Thus acting—we point out their duty to men;
And should the bound-pensioners tell us to hush,
We can throw back the satire, by bidding them
    blush.

Trouble in Boston

BY TERRY FIELAND

If there was trouble, Quincy would be in the middle of it, if not the cause of it. And trouble was brewing that night. Fights between the British soldiers and the townspeople had been breaking out in the streets of Boston for several days. That night seemed to be the worst yet. As for me, I was walking the frozen streets trying to find my son Quincy. He had disobeyed me and gone out with his friends to find redcoats, as the British soldiers were called. Quincy and his friends were only boys, and they were playing a dangerous game. The redcoats were armed and in a bad mood.

The streets were slippery from a heavy snow that had melted and frozen again. The sky was clear and I had a little light from the quarter moon. I came down King Street and saw a crowd of about

Paul Revere made this picture for the *Boston Gazette*. He could have shown soldiers responding to an angry, stone-throwing mob. But as a Patriot, he made it look like a cold-blooded massacre.

fifty men facing less than a dozen British soldiers. The soldiers were guarding the **Custom House**. The crowd was growing larger by the minute. Later reports said there were anywhere from one hundred to five hundred people in the crowd. I hardly noticed, so intent was I on finding my son. I knew he would be there.

The soldiers were firing into the crowd! My heart stopped.

Someone had been ringing the fire bells. That brought people out into the streets. More men came from the docks to see what was going on. And there were boys Quincy's age pushing to the front of the crowd.

People were shoving and cursing the soldiers, throwing things, and daring the redcoats to fire. Just as I got close, one of the redcoats did fire. There was a pause, and then more shots. The soldiers were firing into the crowd! My heart stopped. I could just imagine my boy lying there with a British **musket** ball through him. I knew he would be up front. There men were falling to the ground. The firing did not last long. Maybe ten or eleven men were hit.

People and Terms to Know

Custom House—building where taxes on goods coming into the colonies were paid to the British.

musket—shoulder gun used from the 1500s through the 1700s.

When the crowd recovered from their shock, people began running in every direction. I stumbled forward and helped lift a big black man from the ground. He appeared to be dead. The fellow next to me, who looked like a sailor, said the dead man was named **Crispus Attucks**. Attucks, he said, was one of the first shot by the British.

As the man was speaking, I suddenly saw my son Quincy running to help those who had fallen. Quincy did not see me until he nearly ran into me. I didn't know whether to hit him or hug him, such were my emotions. I was angry with him for disobeying me and putting his life in danger. At the same time, I was filled with joy and relief. I had been so afraid that he was one of those killed by the redcoats. Soon, others came to help with Attucks, and Quincy and I fell to our knees in the frozen snow. We hugged each other and we both wept.

Finally, he cried, "They shot Samuel. He was right beside me. He is dead for sure. We were only

People and Terms to Know

Crispus Attucks—(c. 1723–1770) Little is known about his life before the night of the Boston Massacre. Most historians say he was black. He may have been a runaway slave, and he may have been a sailor. He is the best-remembered victim of the Boston Massacre, and a monument in his honor stands in the Boston Common.

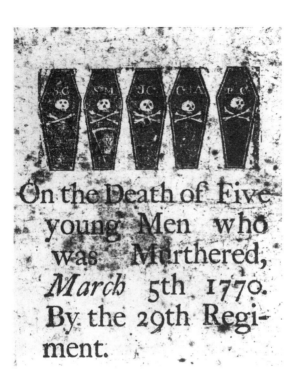

On the Death of Five young Men who was Murthered, March 5th 1770. By the 29th Regiment.

▲
When colonists read about the incident in the paper, they became angrier than ever at the British.

throwing snowballs. We were only throwing snow-balls, and they shot at us."

I couldn't believe that young **Samuel Maverick**, who had spent many hours in our home, was one of those killed. How close I had come to losing my son!

People and Terms to Know

Samuel Maverick—one of the five people killed in the Boston Massacre. He was seventeen. Three of the eleven who were killed or wounded were reported to be the same age.

I put my arm around Quincy as we made our way up King Street toward home. We hardly noticed the people running and shouting all around us. When we got home, I asked a neighbor to inquire about Samuel at the boarding house that his mother kept. I hoped Quincy was wrong, but I feared the worst. Sadly, we were told that young Samuel had been shot and was not expected to live past morning.

None of us slept that night. The next day, Tuesday, the streets were filled with people in a rage. They were shouting their anger over the shooting the night before. Each time the story was told, the number killed by the British grew. It turned out that only five died. There would certainly have been more bloodshed if **Governor Hutchinson** had not given in to Sam Adams and ordered the soldiers moved out of Boston.

*   *   *

Things have been quieter now since the troops left. **Captain Preston** and the eight soldiers who

---

People and Terms to Know

Governor Hutchinson—Thomas Hutchinson (1711–1780), governor of the Massachusetts Colony at the time of the Boston Massacre. The governor was appointed by the British.

Captain Preston—Thomas Preston, officer in charge of the British troops at the Boston Massacre. He was charged with murder but found "not guilty" in the trial that followed.

---

fired into the crowd remain in jail, awaiting trial. **John Adams**, a good lawyer, has agreed to defend them. Adams does not want the British soldiers here in Boston any more than his cousin Sam does. Still, he believes the soldiers deserve a fair trial.

He now sounds more like a man than a boy.

There were a few days after that terrible night when Quincy sounded like his old self. Once I heard him cursing the lobsterbacks, as he calls the British soldiers. He even boasted that he had landed some well aimed snowballs that night and that most of the snowballs had a good hard rock inside.

More recently, though, Quincy speaks of the so-called massacre in a more sober voice. He is still upset over the death of his friend, Samuel Maverick, and talks of him often. All in all, being in the midst of that bloodshed and death has changed him. He now sounds more like a man than a boy. That night was horrible for him, but I think my son will be all right.

People and Terms to Know

John Adams—(1735–1826) American Patriot and the second president of the United States. John Adams and Samuel Adams (see page 45) were cousins.

Together we have had a bitter laugh or two over the drawing by **Paul Revere**. Everybody wants a copy of his picture. "The Bloody Massacre"—that's what Revere calls it. It will soon be hanging in every home in Boston, and it will continue to feed the anger of the people.

The scene in Revere's picture is not like what Quincy and I saw that night. In the picture, you don't see so much as a club in the hands of the townspeople, and Quincy and I saw plenty of clubs. And Revere shows Captain Preston giving the order to fire while his troops are all lined up in a nice row. It wasn't that neat and tidy. I don't know if *anybody* gave an order to fire, such was the confusion.

Revere's picture of that terrible night is not much different from what we have been reading in pamphlets and posters all over Boston. Many people put the blame all on the British. They will be reminding us for years to come of March 5, 1770, and the "Boston Massacre."

People and Terms to Know

Paul Revere—(1735–1818) gifted engraver and silversmith. He is best remembered for his ride on April 18, 1775, warning the colonists that the British troops were coming.

I'm glad that Quincy doesn't think of himself as one of those innocent men in the crowd that Paul Revere drew. I am afraid that there may well be more bloodshed before this is all over. We will need leaders and heroes. Perhaps my son will be one of them. I have hope for him because he at least knows that terrible night had nothing to do with leadership or heroism.

QUESTIONS TO CONSIDER

1. Why do you think the British soldiers fired on the crowd?

2. Who do you think is to blame for the events on March 5, 1770, in Boston?

3. What do you think would have happened if the soldiers had stayed in Boston after the Massacre?

4. How did Paul Revere's picture influence the people of Boston?

5. How did Revere's picture of the Boston Massacre differ from what the narrator and his son experienced?

Boston Revolts!
by Susan Martins Miller

Kathleen Lankford and her family are living in Boston during difficult times. Her brother Will wants to help the Patriot cause at any cost. Kathleen, on the other hand, is not so sure how she feels—especially when she must decide whether or not to help a wounded soldier.

Crispus Attucks:
Black Leader of Colonial Patriots
by Gray Morrow

Crispus Attucks was one of the first people to die in the Revolution when he was shot at the Boston Massacre. What was his life like before he started protesting the British taxes and policy toward the American colonies? Gray Morrow writes about how Crispus Attucks escaped slavery and moved to Boston.

A Spy in the King's Colony
By Lisa Banim

Emily Parker's family are Patriots in 1775 Boston, but their neighbors, the Babcocks, are Loyalists. The problem is that the Babcocks' son Robert says he is a Patriot. Emily and Robert find themselves with the important job of getting a message to General George Washington. Now Emily wonders if Robert is really a spy for the Loyalists.

The Boston Tea Party

BY MARY KATHLEEN FLYNN

Boston, May 30, 1773

Dearest Sister Abigail,

I hope you are enjoying your stay with Aunt Mary and Uncle John. Virginia seems so far away! It has been just a week since you left and I miss you already. Things will be very dull here in Boston without you.

All Mother and Father seem to talk about lately is politics. At supper tonight, Father was very upset about tea, of all things. There are half a million pounds of tea on the way to Boston from Britain. I like tea, so that sounds like a good thing to me. But Father thinks it's a crime!

The Boston Tea Party: Colonists dressed as Native Americans dump British tea into Boston Harbor. Other colonists cheer from the dock.

You should have heard the terrible things Father said about **King George**. Father is angry because the **East India Company**, which is bringing the tea, won't have to pay any taxes on it. Father says the East India Company should have to pay taxes, just like the companies here in Boston have to pay taxes. I must say, I think he's right. It doesn't sound fair to me.

I will write to you when I can. But Father says I can't write too often because King George has put taxes on everything. Even stamps!

Your fond sister,
Anne

*   *   *

November 27, 1773

My dear sister,

Today three ships sailed into Boston Harbor from Britain. They are called the *Dartmouth*, the *Eleanor,* and the *Beaver*. They are docked at Griffin's Wharf. They are full of tea, but the people at Griffin's Wharf will not let them unload it.

People and Terms to Know

King George—George III, king of England from 1760 until 1820, during the time when the American colonies gained independence from England.
East India Company—world's largest trading company at one time.

Father told Mother that the tea will never be unloaded in Boston. He is very angry about something he calls "taxation without representation." Mother told me it means that here in the colonies we have to pay taxes to Great Britain, even though we don't get to vote. I agree with Father. Taxation without representation isn't fair!

Father talks about Samuel Adams as if he is the wisest man in the world.

After dinner tonight, Father went to a special meeting at the Old South Meeting House. At first I thought it was funny to see Father sneaking out of the house at night. But Mother says it is very serious. She says Father and many of his friends are "Sons of Liberty." She is very proud of Father.

The leader of the Sons of Liberty is Samuel Adams. Remember him? He was always starting one company after another. None of them ever did very well. I always thought Father felt a little sorry for him, but now Father talks about Samuel Adams as if he is the wisest man in the world.

I wonder what will happen to those three ships. I wonder what will happen to all that tea!

Your loving sister,
Anne

* * *

December 17, 1773

Dear Abigail,

You would not believe what happened here in Boston last night. Father was part of it, and I watched the whole thing.

Father and the other Sons of Liberty were getting more and more angry about all that tea sitting in the harbor. Governor Hutchinson said the tea should be unloaded. But Samuel Adams and many of the other men, including father, disagreed.

They wanted to talk to Governor Hutchinson about it. He promised to talk to them at five o'clock. They waited all day. But when five o'clock came, the governor wasn't there. He had gone to his country house, six miles away! What a coward, don't you think?

Well, as you can imagine, this made the Sons of Liberty even more angry. A crowd of thousands gathered at the Old South Meeting House to hear Sam Adams give a speech. He demanded that the ships leave and take their **cargo** with them. When the

---

People and Terms to Know

cargo—goods carried by a ship or other vehicle.

The Boston Tea Party   **69**

▲
A colonist dumps tea into the harbor in protest.

meeting broke up, some of the people yelled, "Boston Harbor's a teapot tonight!" Others yelled, "Let every man do his duty, and be true to his country."

While Sam Adams was speaking, Father came home and changed his clothes. When he was ready to go out again, he looked like a Mohawk Indian. He carried a small axe that looked like an Indian tomahawk. And he had painted his face and hands with chimney soot.

He said he was going to Griffin's Wharf, where the three ships with the tea are docked. Father ran to the harbor, and Mother and I followed more slowly. Along the way, Father stopped at a blacksmith's shop. There he met up with a large group of men. They, too, were dressed like Indians. There must have

Two by two, the men dressed as Indians marched quietly to the docks.

been about 200 of them. Their faces were so smeared with coal dust and paint that we couldn't recognize anyone.

The streets were lined with people, but nobody said a word. It was very quiet. Two by two, the men dressed as Indians marched quietly to the docks. Most of the men carried clubs as well as axes.

When the men reached the docks, they divided up into three groups. Each group went onto a ship. Nothing happened for a few moments. I held Mother's hand and waited, wondering what Father and the Sons of Liberty would do.

Then I heard the sounds of chopping wood. Next, I heard a splash, and then another splash, and then another and another. Then men were throwing the chests of tea into Boston Harbor! First they cut up the chests with their axes and then they threw the pieces—tea and all—into the sea. Father told us that they did it so that nobody would be able to use the tea.

The only sounds I could hear were the chopping and the splashing. The men didn't speak. And neither did the thousands of people watching on shore.

I was afraid the governor's men would arrest Father and the Sons of Liberty. There were British armed ships all over the harbor, but nobody tried to stop the Sons of Liberty. Later, I heard that the British admiral, Admiral Montague, watched the whole thing from his house.

I was up way past my bedtime. It took about three hours for the Sons of Liberty to throw all the chests of tea overboard. It was nine o'clock by the time the men were finished. Father told me there were more than 340 chests of tea! I bet the East India Company and King George will be angry.

By the way, the tea was the only thing the men destroyed on the three ships! When they finished, they swept the decks clean and put everything back in its place.

When the Sons of Liberty finished throwing the tea overboard, they walked quietly away from the wharf. It was a beautiful sight. There they all were, still dressed as Indians, resting their axes on their shoulders. Somebody played a **fife**. When they walked past Admiral Montague's house, he yelled out to them, "Well boys, you have had a fine, pleasant evening for your Indian **caper**, haven't you? But mind, you have got to pay the fiddler yet!"

Father and Mother are both very happy that the **Boston Tea Party**, as people are calling it, went so well. But I must say I'm worried about what the admiral might do to Father and the Sons of Liberty. And what about King George? How will he get back at the people of Boston?

As always, your fond sister,
Anne

* * *

King George III did indeed get back at the people of Boston. He closed the port of Boston and put

---

People and Terms to Know

fife—small flute.

caper—wild prank.

Boston Tea Party—event on the evening of December 16, 1773, when the people of Boston threw chests of tea overboard to protest against Great Britain.

British soldiers all over town. But that only made the people of Boston more angry. The Boston Tea Party was one of the events that led to the Revolutionary War.

QUESTIONS TO CONSIDER

1. Why were the people of Boston angry about the East India Company?

2. Why did the Sons of Liberty throw the tea into Boston Harbor?

3. What would you have felt and what would you have done if you'd been in Boston on the night of December 16, 1773?

4. How did King George get back at the people of Boston?

A Secret Party in Boston Harbor
by Kris Hemphill

Eleven-year-old Sarah Turner sees the Boston Massacre and escapes without harm. She also helps with the Boston Tea Party. She decides to find out who has been disloyal to the Patriots. Will her luck hold out?

Boston Tea Party: Rebellion in the Colonies
by James E. Knight

This book tells what it was like to live during the days just before the Revolutionary War began. The times were very tense, and James E. Knight captures the worries and hopes of the people who were part of the early days of the Revolution.

The Boston Tea Party
by Steven Kroll

If you like art, then you will love this book. Steven Kroll describes the characters and the action in each picture. The pictures give you another way of seeing how other people look at how and why the American Revolution started.

Common Sense
Changes Minds

BY STEPHEN CURRIE

Trenton, New Jersey
December 8, 1775

"It's a chilly day," observed John Hastings, seating himself at the table and rubbing his red hands together briskly. "I fear there is more of the same ahead."

"They say it shall be a hard winter," his wife Elizabeth murmured. She placed a steaming bowl of stew before her husband. "There, my dear, this will warm you."

John gripped the hot bowl in his hands. "It smells delicious," he said, inhaling the warm scent of meat, carrots, turnips, and potatoes. "I am sure it will taste the same."

"Thank you, kind sir," said Elizabeth, dropping into her own seat across the small wooden table

Mealtime in the days leading up to the American Revolution was a time to

from John. She smoothed her skirts and smiled. "Four months after our wedding, I am delighted that my husband still compliments my cookery."

John swallowed a spoonful of the stew. "It's better than ever," he pronounced. "Tell me, what manner of man does not compliment his wife's cookery?"

A man who does not wish to be fed, Elizabeth thought, but all she said was: "There are those who do not. I saw Sarah Sharpe in the market last week. She told me that her husband likes nothing that she makes."

"Caleb Sharpe is a stubborn goat of a man who must always be in the right," John said.

Elizabeth dipped her own spoon into her bowl, her eyes dancing. She had known her own beloved husband to be something of a stubborn goat himself. "Truth to tell," she admitted, "poor Sarah might be more sparing with the salt."

"'Tis a family tradition in the Sharpe household, I believe," John said. "Caleb, in his turn, could be more sparing with his talk."

Elizabeth raised an eyebrow. "What do you mean?"

John pushed a chunk of bread into the gravy. "Caleb has cast his lot with the rebels up Massachusetts way—the ones who think America ought to be an independent nation, free from England." His lip curled.

"It is a thought," said Elizabeth, and she felt her pulse quicken.

John snorted. "Such thoughts are treason. We are English. We may live here in the colonies, but England is our mother country." He lifted a spoonful of stew to his lips. Wood crackled in the fireplace behind him. "Caleb Sharpe can't be swayed by reason."

"We are English. We may live here in the colonies, but England is our mother country."

"And yet," said his wife slowly, twisting a curl of hair around her finger, "you were born here in New Jersey. Your father, and my father as well, were born here. We have never set foot in England."

"But we are English for all of that," returned John. "George is our king, and we are his loyal subjects. Even you, a woman, ought to know that." He tipped his head to the side, a question in his eyes. "*Do* you know that?"

Elizabeth looked angry. "I am no rebel," she said simply. "I only ask whether the king has our best interests in mind. England is a long way off, and he may not know our needs—"

Common Sense *Changes Minds* 79

"Then we shall tell him," John interrupted, "as we have done in the past. We told him how we disliked the Stamp Act, and he listened. Besides, he protects us from foreign enemies. Do you wish the **French** to take control? The **Spanish**?"

"No," agreed his wife, "but—"

"This talk of independence is foolishness." John banged down his spoon. "'Tis only rabble-rousers in Boston and stubborn goats such as Caleb Sharpe who support the notion. *Thinking* Americans believe no such thing. True, the king has made missteps. No ruler is perfect. Still, there is no justification, no cause to raise an army and to fight." Excited, he stood and gestured with an arm. "Men died on the battlefields of **Lexington** and **Bunker Hill**! What did they die for?"

"John," said Elizabeth calmly.

Her husband slowly lowered his arm. Sheepishly, he sat. "I am sorry, my dear, but my

---

People and Terms to Know

French—government of France. The French tried to gain control of North America in the 1750s. In 1763, they were defeated by the English and the American colonists in the French and Indian war.

Spanish—government of Spain. At the time of the American Revolution, Florida and much of the land west of the Mississippi River belonged to Spain.

Lexington—Battles of Lexington and Concord on April 19, 1775, marked the beginning of the Revolutionary War. The battle started when 70 Patriots challenged a British patrol on its way to Concord to seize the rebels' military supplies. Eight colonists died, and ten were wounded.

Bunker Hill—Battle of Bunker Hill. It was fought near Boston in June 1775. The British won, but they had 1,054 casualties. The Patriots had 450.

point still stands. Troubled as these times may be, the solution is not violence. We are English; let us not fight our father and mother." He picked up his spoon. "This would show a lack of—of—"

"Of common sense?" asked Elizabeth.

"Exactly," agreed John.

*　　*　　*

Trenton, New Jersey
March 24, 1776

"'T is cold outside," complained John, seating himself at the table and removing his heavy boots. "I thank you kindly for the warm fire."

"I thought spring was on its way," Elizabeth said, "but it seems to have been delayed." She served her husband his meat and vegetables and filled his cup. "What was the news today in town?"

John sipped his drink. "All good," he said. "Our rebels have taken Boston. I heard it directly from Caleb Sharpe. The king's armies have left the town altogether, and the field of operations now moves to New York."

"'Tis good news indeed!" Elizabeth leaned forward across the table. "Husband," she said softly, "are you glad now that Caleb gave you that pamphlet to read?"

"*Common Sense*?" John chewed his meat. "Aye, that I am. He wrote so clearly, so thoughtfully, did our good **Mr. Paine**. He attacked kings, and argued how wicked it is to have a government of kings."

"He attacked kings, and argued how wicked it is to have a government of kings."

"Kings have 'laid the world in blood and ashes,'" murmured Elizabeth, who had read the little pamphlet again and again. "So writes Mr. Paine."

"Yes," John said. "He wrote about England's reasons for protecting us, which have little to do with our own safety and everything to do with protecting her own trade."

"'She would have defended Turkey based on the same motive,'" Elizabeth quoted.

"She would." John sampled a bean. "He noted the king's unwillingness to listen to our pleas."

Elizabeth continued to quote *Common Sense*. "'From Britain we can expect nothing but ruin.'"

People and Terms to Know

Common Sense—famous pamphlet that persuaded many Americans a complete break with England was necessary. It was written by Thomas Paine and published in January 1776.

Mr. Paine—Thomas Paine (1737–1809), Englishman who immigrated to America before the Revolution. He was the author of *Common Sense*.

▲

Thomas Paine, author of *Common Sense*.

John nodded. "Aye. The truth is, my dear, that we are not Englishmen; we are Americans. Why, most of us here in New Jersey have no connection to England. I was born in the colonies, as was my father, and yours too." He picked up the loaf of bread that Elizabeth had baked earlier in the day.

"I was aware of that," said Elizabeth, choking back a laugh. "I am glad you no longer think we are Englishmen."

"I never thought we were anything but Americans," John said, narrowing his eyes. "And before you should ask, I never opposed independence either, nor supported the king in his foul treatment of us."

"Ah!" said Elizabeth, smiling inwardly and thinking of stubborn old goats. "Then Thomas Paine did nothing to change your mind and your heart."

"He did nothing whatever." John pulled gently at one end of the bread. "He merely put into words what I and many others had been thinking all along, that—how did he say it—"

"That 'the blood of the slain, the weeping voice of nature cries 'TIS TIME TO PART,'" Elizabeth said.

"Aye," said John, tugging harder. "What he wrote was sweet and simple and filled with—with—"

"With common sense?" asked Elizabeth.

"Exactly," John said as he tore the loaf of bread into two pieces.

QUESTIONS TO CONSIDER

1. What did Elizabeth think about independence in the first scene of the story?

2. What does the story tell you about the role of women during Revolutionary times in America?

3. What were some of the arguments against independence that John offered in the story? Which seem to you to be the most effective?

4. How did the publication of *Common Sense* change the way Americans thought about England and independence?

5. What do you think Thomas Paine meant when he wrote, "The blood of the slain, the weeping voice of nature cries 'TIS TIME TO PART"?

This paragraph is from Thomas Paine's *Common Sense*. Notice the language he uses. He compares the king of England to a "sullen-tempered Pharaoh" and later calls him "a wretch." Why does he use this language? The events he refers to on "the fatal nineteenth of April, 1775" are the battles at Lexington and Concord—the start of the Revolutionary War.

No man was a warmer wisher for a [renewed friendship with England] than myself, before the fatal nineteenth of April, 1775, but the moment the event of that day was made known, I rejected the hardened, sullen-tempered Pharaoh of England forever . . . the wretch, that with the pretended title of Father of His People can unfeelingly hear of their slaughter, and [calmly] sleep with their blood upon his soul.

The Revolutionary War

part two

The Battle
of Saratoga

BY WALTER HAZEN

"Well, it sounds like you put a right smart whipping on them, Caleb. And you say your outfit captured **General Burgoyne** himself?"

Mr. Dandridge wanted to know everything about the battle. Poor fellow; they said he was too old to enlist when the war began. He really hated having to stay behind when we young fellows marched off to fight the British.

"We sure did," I replied to his question. "In fact, Captain Morris told me we captured seven of those redcoat generals. In all, about 5,000 redcoats and

---

People and Terms to Know

General Burgoyne—(1722–1792) British officer whose defeat at the Battle of Saratoga was the turning point of the war. He was called "Gentleman Johnny" because he was a member of fashionable society, a politician, and a playwright in addition to being a soldier.

British General Burgoyne's surrender at the Battle of Saratoga marks the
point in the war when the Americans began to win.

Hessians threw down their guns and surrendered at Saratoga."

"What did they do with all those prisoners?" Mr. Dandridge asked.

"Gentleman Johnny wanted to capture the area around the Hudson River."

"I don't know," I answered. "I heard they were planning to march them to Boston and put them on ships for England. The captain said they'd have to swear they wouldn't come back to fight again."

Mr. Dandridge wanted the full story of the big battle at Saratoga, New York. I explained that it all began in July 1777. That's when "Gentleman Johnny" Burgoyne moved south out of Canada with about 8,000 men. This number included Hessian troops and about 80 Indians.

"Where were they headed?" Mr. Dandridge asked.

"Albany," I replied. "Gentleman Johnny wanted to capture the area around the Hudson River. That would cut New England and New York off from

---

People and Terms to Know

Hessians—soldiers from Germany hired by the British to fight against the Americans in the Revolutionary War.

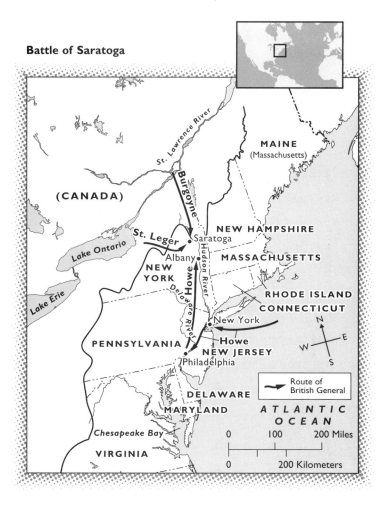

Battle of Saratoga

the other colonies. Captain Morris said it was all part of a three-pronged British attack intended to end the war."

"What's a three-pronged attack?" Mr. Dandridge asked.

"Well, the Captain explained it this way. Burgoyne was supposed to come down from

Canada and meet up with **Howe**. Howe's army was moving up from New York City. A third, smaller group led by a colonel named St. Leger was supposed to move into Albany from the west. The British figured if all three groups got to Albany at the same time, they could lick us good."

"So, what happened?" asked Mr. Dandridge. "Something must have gone wrong."

"That's for sure," I said. "The group coming from the west got whipped along the way and never made it to Albany. Then, General Howe decided to attack Philadelphia before he hightailed it to Albany to help Burgoyne. So, Burgoyne was left pretty much on his own."

"What did he do?" Mr. Dandridge continued. "Burgoyne had to go on with his attack, didn't he?"

"He did," I replied, "and I guess that was about the biggest mistake he ever made. He attacked on September 19, but he didn't know we were ready for him. **General Gates** had us waiting high up on a hill above the Hudson. Some of us were hidden really well in the underbrush and the treetops."

People and Terms to Know

Howe—Sir William Howe (1729–1814), Commander-in-Chief of British forces in America from 1776 to 1778.

General Gates—General Horatio Gates (1727–1808), American commander at the Battle of Saratoga in New York.

"You must have really surprised him," Mr. Dandridge said.

"*Shocked* might be a better word," I drawled. "Colonel Dan Morgan used a turkey hunter's lure to give us the signal to fire. When the redcoats got really close, he gave it a blare or two."

Gobblegobblegobblegobble.

Mr. Dandridge roared with laughter. He laughed so hard that he nearly fell over.

"You should've seen the looks on the faces of those redcoats," I continued. "In no time at all, we picked off about 600 of them. Yes sir, it was like a regular turkey shoot!"

Mr. Dandridge finally contained himself, although just thinking about the sound of the turkey hunter's lure still made him smile.

"Well, Caleb," he said, "you must have felt pretty proud of yourself, after that battle. It seems to have persuaded the French we could win this war."

"Heck no," I answered. "At the time, I didn't know that it would help the French decide to come into the war on our side. I was thinking about the next battle. We knew the redcoats would attack again. And sure enough, they attacked just a couple of weeks later. But by that time, we had them outnumbered.

"The hero of that battle was **Benedict Arnold**," I said. "I'll tell you, Mr. Dandridge, I never saw anything like it. The redcoats were marching across this wheat field when we let them have it good. In the middle of all that commotion, I saw General Arnold riding back and forth on his horse, waving

"Those redcoats took off running like a bunch of scared jackrabbits."

his sword in the air, and yelling for the boys to follow him. And they did! Those redcoats took off running like a bunch of scared jackrabbits. The general ended up getting shot in the leg, but he waved to all the boys as he was carried away on a stretcher. I'll tell you one thing: he was a hero to us all."

"And the British gave up right after that?" Mr. Dandridge asked.

"Pretty soon afterwards," I answered. "They skedaddled up to Saratoga, just a little way to the north, as you know. The Captain said that by mid-October, they were fairly done in. They were low on food and supplies, and we had them way

People and Terms to Know

Benedict Arnold—(1741–1801) American major general who played a leading role in the Battle of Saratoga. He later turned traitor and fought for the British.

▲

A wounded General Arnold tries to rise from his fallen horse.

outnumbered. Burgoyne had little choice but to call it quits. On October 17, he handed his sword to General Gates and surrendered."

"Well," Mr. Dandridge sighed, "it's pretty clear that I missed out on something big. That battle at Saratoga made France get off the fence and decide to help us. Now with France sending over soldiers and ships, maybe we'll win this thing after all."

"It looks better than it did a few months ago," I agreed. "But we still have a long way to go."

QUESTIONS TO CONSIDER

1. What was General Burgoyne's plan to bring the war to a quick end?

2. Why did General Burgoyne's plan fail?

3. What role did Benedict Arnold play in the British defeat at Saratoga?

4. How did the Battle of Saratoga prove to be the turning point of the war?

Lexington and Concord
by Deborah Kent

While the Battle of Saratoga was the beginning of the end of the war, the battles at Lexington and Concord started it and set the tone for battle. Just to get people from all thirteen colonies willing to fight against the British was a challenge. These battles helped unite the colonies in their fight for independence.

The Minute Boys of Bunker Hill
by Edward Stratemeyer

Roger feels it is his duty to fight for independence, and nothing will stop him from joining the fight at Bunker Hill outside Boston. War is never easy, and Roger survives fierce fighting, prison, and the stress of army life to continue the fight.

Saratoga
by David C. King

This book describes the Battle of Saratoga and tells how the Patriots won in the end. The battle was very important for the American colonies because it was such a big victory for their side. David C. King also tells how you can visit the battlegrounds today.

Valley Forge

BY BRIAN J. MAHONEY

It was a rainy January day in 1778 when John Morris, a young man in British-occupied **Philadelphia**, made an important decision. He decided to leave his home and job to join General George Washington's army in the War of Independence.

Washington had failed to stop Sir William Howe and his British thugs from taking over John's beloved city. Now the redcoats marched through the streets as if they owned them! John was disgusted by

---

People and Terms to Know

Philadelphia—city in Pennsylvania that was the nation's capital before Washington, D.C. The Continental Congress met in Philadelphia.

General Washington and Lafayette riding through Valley Forge. Cold, hungry soldiers wait out the winter at Valley Forge.

the way the proud <u>Tories</u> welcomed these British trespassers. They threw parties for them and even took the officers to the theater.

John stood at the hospital window, watching the red blocks of soldiers pass, and his anger boiled over. "No!" he said. "The colonies do not exist only to serve mother England!"

"Calm down, John," said his mother, coming up behind him. "You can do more good by tending to our patients than by shouting at the British." Plump and energetic Mary Morris had been running the small hospital since her husband's death ten years ago.

John had grown up among the sick. He had helped his mother tend to births, deaths, and everything in between. It had seemed natural for John to follow in his parents' footsteps. He'd left home just long enough to complete his medical studies. Then he'd returned to help his mother run the hospital. But now John couldn't help feeling that his skills would be more useful on the battlefield than in this tiny Philadelphia hospital.

People and Terms to Know

Tories—Loyalists, colonists who supported continued rule by Great Britain. *Tory* comes from an Irish slang word meaning "robber" or "outlaw." Like the Patriots, Tories were against taxation without representation, but they feared the violence and disorder that could result from overturning the government.

Of course, his mother wanted him to stay. Her only interest in the Revolution was to keep her son clear of it.

But it just wasn't enough for John to watch the War for Independence from his quiet hospital window. One night, after leaving his patients in the care of another doctor, he packed his knapsack and left a short goodbye letter on his mother's chair:

Her only interest in the Revolution was to keep her son clear of it.

D earest Mother,

I think you have known for some time that I would one day be leaving to do my part for the Revolution. The time has now come. I know you will be safe here, and that you can manage well without me while I am away.

As for me, I plan to join up with General Washington's troops at their **winter quarters**. Rest

---

People and Terms to Know

winter quarters—place where the army stayed during the winter months, when they stopped fighting. British soldiers usually did not fight in cold and snow. They would set up camp for the winter in or near large cities. In the winter of 1777–1778, General Howe's troops took over Philadelphia. They were celebrating recent victories over George Washington at Brandywine Creek and at Germantown. George Washington chose Valley Forge, 20 miles northwest of Philadelphia, for winter quarters because it was close enough to Philadelphia that he could keep an eye on the British, but far enough away that they couldn't launch a surprise attack.

assured that my skills as a surgeon will be put to good use in the service of the Continental Army. I will write to you often, and pray that when I return, the redcoats will be gone from our dear city!

Your loving son,
John

*   *   *

John shivered as he made his way along the muddy roads toward General Washington's winter camp at Valley Forge. He had learned that the camp was located on high ground near a few important roadways outside of Philadelphia.

The countless American wagons buried in the mud along the roadway puzzled him. "Maybe it's a defensive measure," he thought. As his horse plodded on through the muck, John thought of what lay ahead of him. He imagined glorious scenes of a brave young doctor bringing proud and bloody men back to life.

Outside of Valley Forge, a band of ragtag soldiers challenged him.

"Halt! Sir, are you a loyal British subject?" asked a black-toothed man from behind a musket barrel.

"No. My loyalty lies with the colonies and against tyranny," John replied. "I am a surgeon who wishes to join your noble cause."

"Thank you, kind sir, but we're not feeling very noble at the moment!" joked a filthy soldier in a tattered uniform. The group coughed and twisted with laughter as they waved John into the camp. One of the guards coughed out directions to a hut where he could to sign up.

He bit his lip and thought, Oh, Mother, I've made a mistake!

Were those Continental soldiers or prisoners on the loose, John wondered. His eyes widened as he entered the huge, mud-filled camp. The smell was awful. The noise was worse. Scattered around him were fighting men of all ages and walks of life—white men, black men, and Indians. The thousands of muddy souls milling about created an unceasing groan. Dirty, half-naked men eyed him hungrily as he passed, begging for his clothes and food.

John's patriotism began to falter, and a great fear began to grow within him. He bit his lip and thought, Oh, Mother, I've made a mistake!

Then John noticed a little shack, about 15 by 25 feet, with the word *Hospital* written on it. He got off his horse, held it (lest someone steal it and eat it!), and approached the hut.

"Can I be of service?" offered a voice behind him. John turned to find an officer in a blackened uniform smiling at him.

"Yes, pardon me, but I'm here to enlist as a surgeon, and . . ."

The man laughed. "Ah, and have you made yourself at home yet?"

"Why, no, sir," John confessed.

"Well, you're looking at a surgeon! My name is Waldo, **Dr. Albigence Waldo**. And I must tell you that this can be a difficult place for a gentleman without a proper introduction! Join me for lunch?"

John introduced himself and joined Waldo on the cold hospital steps. Lunch for the two, John quickly realized, was going to have to come from his own knapsack. He silently watched as this cultured man—a doctor no less—devoured John's **mutton** and bread!

"When we arrived here in early December, I had hoped that the army could rest, train, and get its health back." Waldo said between mouthfuls.

People and Terms to Know

Dr. Albigence Waldo—(1750–1794) surgeon at Valley Forge whose diary contained detailed accounts of the army's sufferings.

mutton—meat from a full-grown sheep.

"But the lack of drink, food, and basic supplies soon changed my feelings! We pitched our tents far away from all the pleasures and enjoyments of the city! Now most of us are starving, sick, and in need of clothing. You'll find that some of the officers are better off—but NOT this one!"

Waldo laughed heartily, coughed, and grew serious. "Truthfully, son, we are all in desperate need, and, if it weren't for the character of that man George Washington, this army would surely fall apart! Of course he knows that we could occupy a city and enjoy its comforts, but that would make us easy targets for a British attack. This camp is in a safe place, but it is terribly hard on the men."

"But, isn't Washington responsible for improving these frightful conditions?" John asked.

"It's not that simple, son. The **quartermaster** general, Thomas Mifflin, was in charge of supplying us, but he resigned before we arrived here. The word is that the **Continental Congress** isn't responding to Washington's pleas for help. Perhaps the Congress is angry that the British forced it to flee

---

People and Terms to Know

quartermaster—person who oversees army supplies.

Continental Congress—group of men who officially represented and acted for the various colonies, first in 1774 (First Continental Congress), and later 1775–1781 (Second Continental Congress).

George Washington inspects his troops in the bitter cold at Valley Forge. This painting is by American artist N. C. Wyeth (1882–1945).

from Philadelphia! Now, dishonest soldiers and **civilians** steal much of the food, clothes, and medicines we need."

"Is the army out of money?" John asked, fearing the answer.

People and Terms to Know

civilians—people not in the military.

"Have you heard the expression, 'Not worth a **Continental**'? British money has a more trusted value, and the honest men who try to buy supplies for us find that farmers and shopkeepers are afraid to take our currency! It's safer to sell to the British, and many do, I'm afraid. It angers me to no end. Imagine! The very people we are fighting for refuse to support us, and then they complain openly about us!

"It's safer to sell to the British, and many do, I'm afraid."

"We send out parties to **forage** from nearby farms, and found that the British and American armies have already stolen it! The result is that good men must remain sick, starving, cold, unwashed, and unclothed. But we still perform like soldiers, building huts on the warm side of hills and watching for a redcoat attack."

Just then John noticed an almost naked man staring at them from the hospital doorway, at the

---

People and Terms to Know

Continental—money issued by the Continental Congress in 1775 to fund the war. Citizens lost confidence as more money was printed than Congress could actually back up with gold and silver. If Britain won the war, the Continental currency would be worthless, and people often refused to accept it.

forage—search for food.

top of the steps. "Pardon me, doctor, but do you have any **firecake**?"

Waldo removed what looked like a clump of blackened earth from his pocket, and, climbing the steps, gave it to a man he called Samuel.

"Come in, John," Waldo said.

John followed him up the steps and through the door. He couldn't believe what he saw. The smoky hut was filled with patients in rags, lying on the bare poles of their bunks.

"We have no straw for beds and hardly any medical supplies. You'd be surprised how healthy we were when we had mutton and **grog** on Christmas Eve! Now we're either choking on **greenwood** smoke to stay warm or freezing to death outside.

"I mostly tend to cases with the itch, various fevers, smallpox, pneumonia, and frostbite so bad that I have to perform regular amputations." Waldo shook his head slowly. "Samuel here has sold his

---

People and Terms to Know

firecake—small bread or roll made of meal and water and cooked over an open fire.

grog—drink of rum diluted with water.

greenwood—freshly cut damp wood that creates a lot of smoke as it burns.

clothes for food, and now he's well but he can't leave unless he gets some clothes!"

John had had enough of all the sickness and misery around him. He quickly thanked the doctor and made for the door.

"Where are you going, John?" Waldo asked. "Home," John whispered. The word had the effect of a musket shot, startling the ragged bodies, who rose up in their beds and stared at the frightened young surgeon.

As John looked at the eyes of the sick and wounded, he began to understand. The tattered souls around him had volunteered to sacrifice all their comforts, their humanity—everything—to fight for freedom and the right to go home. After so much misery, every moment was filled with their longing for home—but they would not abandon Washington until King George couldn't bully them, tax them, or imprison them anymore.

*   *   *

John decided to remain at Valley Forge, where he cured itches, cut away limbs, cared for the sick, and mourned the dead. His kind spirit, like that of his mother, earned him many friends and admirers.

Months later, Mary Morris received a letter from her son:

Dearest Mother,

We're moving out of Valley Forge. A German officer named **Baron von Steuben** has turned our rough Continental Army into a professional fighting unit! And last year's victory at Saratoga finally convinced the French to openly join our cause! Don't worry, I'll be home as soon as the British go home!

Love,
John

QUESTIONS TO CONSIDER

1. What was life like for the British who occupied Philadelphia in the winter of 1777–1778?

2. Who were the Tories and how did they treat the British occupiers?

3. Why did Washington camp at Valley Forge?

4. What were the main causes of suffering at Valley Forge?

5. How had the army changed by the time it left Valley Forge?

People and Terms to Know

Baron von Steuben—(1730–1794) German general who helped turn George Washington's army into a well-trained fighting force.

A Young Patriot: The American Revolution as Experienced by One Boy
by Jim Murphy

Joseph Plumb Martin is only 15, yet he is fighting for the Patriots in the army. The army is not as organized as he thought. There are many hardships, and there are even mutinies! Joseph wonders if these troops have what it takes to defeat the British.

Crossing the Delaware: A History in Many Voices
by Louise Peacock

This story of the Revolutionary War uses actual letters to show what soldiers were thinking and feeling when they camped at Valley Forge. Many had lost hope, but these letters show what kept them eager to fight again.

Valley Forge
by R. Conrad Stein

George Washington's troops were defeated at Brandywine, and they were forced to retreat. They stayed at Valley Forge through a harsh winter before going on to win the war. This book has photos of battle sites, quotes from the soldiers and the officers, and lots of information on how the army survived.

The *Bonhomme Richard* Fights the *Serapis*

BY DIANE WILDE

The day was clear and cold, and the waters of the **North Sea** were calm and smooth off the coast of Flamborough Head, a broad ridge of chalk cliffs rising 450 feet above the sea on the northeast coast of England. Centuries of wind and water had carved deep gullies in the cliff walls.

It was September 23, 1779. The American Revolution had been raging for over three years. American captain **John Paul Jones** paced the deck

---

People and Terms to Know

North Sea—body of water that stretches north from the English Channel to the Norwegian Sea. It falls between the east coast of England and the west coasts of Belgium, The Netherlands, Germany, and Denmark.

John Paul Jones—(1747–1792) naval captain of the American Revolution. His famous battle cry, "I have not yet begun to fight," is carved above his tomb.

An artist's impression of the famous sea battle made about 70 years after the event.

of his ship, the ***Bonhomme Richard***, which had been given to him by the king of France earlier that year. Jones had repaired and refitted the old trading ship to serve as a warship.

Jones had three other warships under his command that day, the *Alliance*, the *Pallas*, and the *Vengeance*. He was an officer who never fought by the book. Instead, he made a point of being alert to opportunities as they presented themselves. Jones was known as a tough commander who could lose his temper at times. Some men found it hard to follow him. For this particular military operation, though, he had chosen his own officers and he enjoyed the high regard of his crew.

The wind coming from the southwest was light and variable, which was not good for sailing. At 3:00 P.M. the lookouts sighted 41 British merchant ships sailing north-northeast. These ships were a **convoy** from the Baltic Sea returning to England with supplies for the Royal Navy. They were escorted by two

---

People and Terms to Know

Bonhomme Richard—battleship commanded by John Paul Jones. The ship was given to Jones by the French king and named in honor of Benjamin Franklin, author of *Poor Richard's Almanac*.

convoy—group of ships moving together with one or more escort ships for protection.

warships—the new, copper-bottomed *Serapis*, carrying 50 guns, and the *Countess of Scarborough*, with 20 guns.

Captain Richard Pearson of the Royal Navy commanded the *Serapis*, which was newer, faster, and could turn more quickly than the *Bonhomme Richard*. The *Bonhomme Richard* was not built to fight, but to carry goods between France and the East Indies.

*The **Bonhomme Richard** was not built to fight, but to carry goods between France and the East Indies.*

Jones knew that overtaking this large British convoy would be a great help for the American war effort. This was just the kind of opportunity he had been looking for. Still, he saw that he would have to take or sink the escort ships before he could get at the convoy.

At sunset, Captain Jones gave the signal to prepare for battle. Jones was flying a British flag to allow him to get close to British ships. As the

---

People and Terms to Know

Serapis (suh•RAY•pihs)—British warship. It had three masts, square-rigged sails, and a row of guns along the length of its decks.

Bonhomme Richard came within shouting distance, Captain Pearson of the *Serapis* called out, asking for the ship's name.

"*Princess Royal*," answered the ship's master. "Where from?" Pearson did not hear a response. "Answer immediately or I'll have to fire into you."

At this point, Jones pulled down the **Union Jack** and ran up the American flag. He gave orders to fire a **broadside**. *Serapis* fired at the same time. Two of Jones's guns exploded during the first or second discharge, destroying nearby guns, blowing up the deck above, and killing many of his own sailors. After two or three exchanges of cannon fire, Jones saw that he could not defeat the more heavily armed *Serapis* this way. *Bonhomme Richard* had only forty guns and they were not as powerful as the guns on the *Serapis*. He would have to try to tie the ships together with **grappling irons** and board the *Serapis* for hand-to-hand combat.

Captain Pearson tried to sail across *Richard*'s **bow** to scrape her, but he couldn't build up enough momentum in the light wind. Jones saw what

---

People and Terms to Know

Union Jack—nickname for the British flag.

broadside—shooting of all the guns on one side of a ship at the same time.

grappling irons—iron claws on the ends of ropes used to fasten an enemy ship alongside before boarding.

bow—front section of a ship or boat.

Pearson was trying to do, so he ran *Richard's* bow into *Serapis's* **stern**. Captain Pearson, assuming that Jones was ready to give up, called out, "Has your ship **struck**?"

Jones replied, "I have not yet begun to fight!"

The ships pulled away from each other and straightened out. Helped by a fresh gust of wind, *Richard* surged ahead to cross *Serapis's* bow. The two ships collided bow to stern. They smashed together so that the muzzles of their guns were touching.

"I have not yet begun to fight!"

Jones shouted, "Well done, my brave lads, we have got her now; throw the grappling-irons on board her and stand by for boarding!"

Pearson ordered his men to cast off the grappling-hooks, but French Militia sharpshooters on the deck of the *Richard* prevented them from doing so.

It was now about 8:30 in the evening, and a nearly full harvest moon began to rise in the east. The weather was clear and the ocean surface was

---

People and Terms to Know

stern—rear section of a ship or boat.
struck—pulled down its flag; that is, surrendered.

Moonlit combat between the *Bonhomme Richard* and the *Serapis*.

strangely calm. By this time, English spectators who had heard the big guns were watching the battle from the top of the cliffs at Flamborough Head.

The two ships were locked together in combat. *Serapis* tried to pull away, but couldn't free herself from the grip of the grappling lines. Jones knew that his only chance to defeat the much better armed *Serapis* was to stay at close quarters. There, he could take advantage of the good marksmanship of his French Militia sharpshooters and the bravery of his hard-fighting seamen.

Soon the sails of both ships were on fire and both crews had to stop fighting each other to put out the flames. Meanwhile, the captain of one of Jones's other ships, the *Alliance*, seemed to have gone completely mad. He sailed the *Alliance* around the two grappling ships, shooting broadsides. Unfortunately, he hit the *Bonhomme Richard* instead of the *Serapis,* killing several men and damaging the ship further.

Captain Jones was loading and firing one of his 9-pound guns when he became so exhausted that he had to sit down to rest for a moment. One of his sailors said, "For God's sake, Captain, strike!" Jones jumped up, "No, I will sink. I will never strike."

By 10:00 that night there was water five feet deep in *Richard's* cargo area, at the bottom of the ship. Jones released the prisoners there, gave them buckets, and told them to start emptying the water.

The battle continued for another 30 minutes. The situation seemed hopeless for Jones. His ship was on fire and sinking, and most of his guns were out of commission. *Serapis's* largest guns were still firing. Finally, just before 10:30, the **mainmast** of the *Serapis* began to totter. Captain Pearson, fearing that if it fell, his ship would roll over and sink, decided to give up.

Lieutenant Richard Dale boarded the *Serapis* and brought Captain Pearson aboard the *Bonhomme Richard*. He formally introduced him to Captain Jones, and Pearson handed over his sword in surrender. Jones complimented Pearson for his gallant fight, and the two men went below deck to share a glass of wine. Moments after Pearson surrendered, the mast of the *Serapis* fell overboard.

The battle had lasted three and a half hours. Both ships, especially the *Bonhomme Richard*, were in terrible condition by the end of the fight. For a full day after the battle ended, Jones and his crew tried to save the *Richard*, but by 10:00 P.M. on the 24th of September, Jones gave the order to abandon ship. He took over the *Serapis,* and at 11:00 A.M. on the 25th of September the *Richard* sank, bow first, into the North Sea.

People and Terms to Know

mainmast—tallest mast of a sailing ship; a heavy pole that holds up the largest sail.

*   *   *

Captain Landais was the commander of the *Alliance*, which had fired on the *Bonhomme Richard*. He is said to have admitted afterwards that his actions were deliberate. He had hoped to sink the *Richard*. Then he could take credit himself for the victory over the *Serapis*. Landais was dismissed from the service.

John Paul Jones won the sea battle and captured two British ships, but he didn't accomplish his mission. During the night while the battle was raging, all of the British supply ships escaped. Even so, this battle made John Paul Jones famous in both England and America. The fact that he defeated a bigger, faster ship gave a great boost to the American war effort. After the Revolution ended, America disbanded the Navy. In 1787 Jones went to live in Paris. He commanded Russian Navy ships for two years. Then he returned to Paris, where he died in 1792.

QUESTIONS TO CONSIDER

1. How were the *Bonhomme Richard* and the *Serapis* different as warships?

2. Why did Jones attack the *Serapis*?

3. What is your opinion of Jones's decision to attack the British convoy?

4. What did John Paul Jones mean when he said, "I have not yet begun to fight"?

5. What effect did Jones's victory have for the American cause?

John Paul Jones reported to Benjamin Franklin of the battle against the *Serapis*. Here, he asks for advice on how to punish Captain Landais of the *Alliance* for trying to sink the *Bonhomme Richard*:

Upon the Whole, the captain of the Alliance has behaved so Very Ill in Every respect, that I must complain loudly of his Conduct. He pretends that he is authorized to act independent of my command: I have been taught the Contrary; but Supposing it to be so, his Conduct has been base and unpardonable [not acceptable]. . . . Either Captain Landais or myself is highly Criminal, and one or the other must be punished. I [will not] take any steps With him until I have the advice and [approval] of your Excellency. I have been advised by all the officers of the Squadron to put M. Landais under arrest; but as I have postponed it So long, I Will bear With him a Little Longer until the return of [your reply.]

The Swamp Fox

BY JUDITH CONAWAY

I was the Swamp Fox. Please do not misunderstand me. I know the nickname belongs for all history to my dear husband, General **Francis Marion**. But I, his wife, also was the Swamp Fox, and so were many others. Let me explain what I mean.

The Swamp Fox was a hero of the **War for Independence**. He was no ordinary general, and his men were not regular soldiers. They didn't march in columns in time to the beat of drums.

People and Terms to Know

Francis Marion—(c. 1732–1795) American revolutionary commander known as the Swamp Fox. In 1780, he led a small force of men against the British in South Carolina. They staged surprise attacks, cut British supply lines, and rescued American prisoners. After the war, Marion was elected to the senate of South Carolina.

War for Independence—name for the American Revolution (1775–1783) used by writers of the time.

General Marion takes off through the swamps after a surprise attack

Instead they traveled in small groups, moving silently through forests, fields, and swamps.

The Swamp Fox and his men did not usually fight open battles. They made surprise attacks. They also fought the British by capturing supplies, weapons, and horses and by burning boats and bridges. After each raid or **skirmish**, they would disappear back into the swamps.

The British never understood how the Swamp Fox could be in so many places at once

The British were terrified of the swamps—most people are. These **wetlands** cover vast areas all along the east coast, from Virginia to Florida. You can easily get lost in the mazes of small creeks and islands. Marsh grasses grow higher than your head. There are thick growths of trees: palmetto, pine, oak, and cypress.

My husband knew the swamps of South Carolina like the back of his hand. He hunted and fished in them all his life. He knew the people of the swamps too. Oh, yes, people lived there—they still do. There are Indians, Spaniards, poor whites, and

People and Terms to Know

skirmish—short fight between small groups of soldiers.

wetlands—low-lying areas along coasts and rivers that are flooded for all or part of the year.

Negroes who have run away. You never see most of them, because they do not wish to be seen.

General Marion chose many of his best soldiers from among these people. Many more swamp dwellers took their turns at being the Swamp Fox. They guided our fighters through the swamps and let them stay in their hidden villages. These "invisible people" also formed a huge spy network. The British never understood how the Swamp Fox could be in so many places at once or know so much about them.

Spies were everywhere in those terrible war years. In the South, far more than in the North, the War of Independence was a civil war. Neighbors and even families split into Patriot and **Loyalist** camps. Many people tried to stay out of the war altogether. Some shifted their loyalties back and forth.

The British turned even our slaves and servants against us. They offered freedom to any Negro who went over to their side. As you can imagine, thousands took them up on this offer! South Carolina planters lost at least 20,000 valuable slaves in this manner.

People and Terms to Know

Loyalist—American colonist who remained loyal to King George and opposed independence from Great Britain.

Those of us on the Patriot side supported the Swamp Fox in any way we could. My own Swamp Fox activities involved spying on the best society of South Carolina. We women hear and see far more than men think we do! You might not think that going to picnics, dinners, and balls could be a way to serve one's country. But at social events, men talk about such things as where armies are moving and where supplies are being stored. By listening carefully, I was able to pass on much information of value.

General Marion trusted me completely. We were cousins and had known each other all our lives. Both of us came from old **Huguenot** families. We even looked alike!

For the people of South Carolina, the summer of 1780 was the darkest season of the war. The British captured **Charleston** in May. From Charleston, British troops marched into the interior. General Washington ordered General Gates to come to our defense. The scattered **Continentals**

People and Terms to Know

Huguenot (HYOO•guh•noh)—French Protestant. Many Huguenots left France to escape religious persecution. They were among the first European settlers of South Carolina.

Charleston—port city that is the capital of South Carolina. At the time of the American Revolution, it was the fourth largest city in the colonies, after Philadelphia, New York, and Boston.

Continentals—soldiers who served in the Continental Army, fighting for American independence.

Important Revolutionary Battles in the South

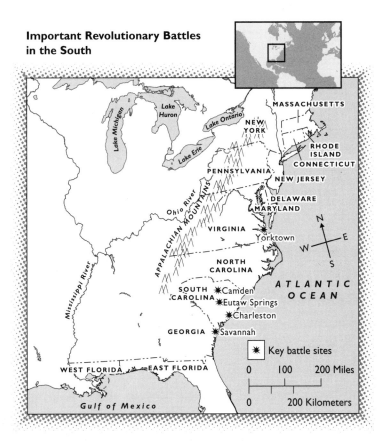

joined the troops Gates was bringing from Maryland and Virginia.

Francis Marion and his men joined Gates in July. Everyone laughed at them. One observer wrote that "their numbers did not exceed twenty men and boys, some white, some black, but most of them miserably equipped." General Gates joined in the general laughter. He didn't even want them in his camp.

On August 16, 1780, British and Continental armies met in battle at **Camden**, South Carolina. It was a terrible defeat for us. When they saw the lines and lines of redcoats, our Continentals panicked and ran. General Gates retreated as quickly as his horse could carry him.

When they saw the lines and lines of redcoats, our Continentals panicked and ran.

Marion had not taken part in the battle of Camden. At the order of General Gates, he and his men were on the Santee River, burning British and Loyalist boats.

When he heard about Camden, he did not tell his men about the defeat. Instead, he led them to Nelson's Ferry, where the British were holding their prisoners. Just four days after the defeat, General Marion and his men made a surprise attack. They killed 23 British soldiers and freed all the prisoners.

In October, General Marion captured a valuable baggage train near Camden. In November he

People and Terms to Know

Camden—town in north-central South Carolina that was the site of a major British victory in the American Revolution.

chased **Colonel Tarleton** and his Green Dragoons into the Ox Swamp. Colonel Tarleton said, "As for the old fox, the Devil himself could not catch him." That's how the legend of the Swamp Fox was born!

In March and April of 1781, General Marion conducted his most brilliant campaigns. By this time he had hundreds of men. He was able to send small groups to many places. They often used the general's favorite battle **tactic**. They would flee as if in defeat, and then turn around and attack the enemy from behind.

In battle after battle, the redcoats declared victory while retreating in panic. The last major British "triumph" was on September 8, 1781, at Eutaw Springs.

Only a few days later, glorious news reached us: French ships had reached the Chesapeake Bay! At last, the help we had been promised had arrived from France! **General Cornwallis**, Colonel Tarleton,

---

People and Terms to Know

Colonel Tarleton—Sir Banastre Tarleton (1754–1833), British officer during the American Revolution known for his cruelty. He was especially hated by the Patriots of South Carolina.

tactic—plan of action.

General Cornwallis—(1738–1805) Charles Cornwallis, British general who led the army in the South and surrendered to the Americans at Yorktown.

and the whole miserable lot of redcoats were ordered north to Virginia. They met their fate there at **Yorktown**. The British surrendered on October 19, 1781.

The fighting did not end right away, of course. There were British troops still scattered around the country. At this time General Marion showed once again his truly noble character. He urged his men to go home to their families and leave the British in peace. He also urged them to be kindly toward those who had been Loyalists. He himself retired from active duty as soon as he could.

The general had lost almost everything he owned in the war. I had been in love with the Swamp Fox for a long time, and we were very close. But he was a shy, proud man, and my wealth was a problem for him. He had such an independent spirit. Finally, though, I made my conquest. We were married in 1786, when I was 49 and he was 54.

People and Terms to Know

Yorktown—town on Chesapeake Bay, in southeastern Virginia, site of the last major battle of the American Revolution.

It was a late marriage, but a good one. I was proud to provide my husband with the fortune that should have been given him by a grateful nation. We lived happily together until his death parted us, on February 27, 1795.

I miss him quite dreadfully. But I am at peace. After all, in the hearts of those who love liberty, the Swamp Fox will never die.

QUESTIONS TO CONSIDER

1. Who was the Swamp Fox? Why was he called that?

2. What does the narrator mean when she says that she, too, was the "Swamp Fox"?

3. How was the Swamp Fox's form of fighting different from ordinary warfare?

4. Why do you think General Marion's way of fighting worked?

A Message for General Washington
by Vivian Schurfranz

Hannah is only 12 when she is asked to deliver an important message to General George Washington. She has to avoid spies on her journey, and she also wants to see her father, who is fighting in Washington's army.

Come All You Brave Soldiers: Blacks in the Revolutionary War
by Clinton Cox

Over 5,000 black men helped the Patriot cause during the Revolution. Even though the British had offered freedom to slaves who joined them, these black soldiers believed in American liberty and independence. Clinton Cox writes about individuals who had important roles in the Revolutionary War.

Yorktown
by Michael Weber

Michael Weber's book describes just how the end came for the British army. The story is told from an officer's view and from the view of ordinary soldiers. The book includes information on visiting these battlefields today.

Life on the
Home Front

BY JANE LEDER

Dorchester, South Carolina

August 28, 1780

My Dear Emily,

I was happy to find that you and your family
are well. I have had a sick headache for many days
now, and I believe it's from worry. If all mothers
whose sons have gone to fight this war against the
British feel as I do, we will be a very ill nation!

The stores here have been raided by the
British soldiers. They have taken food, medicine,
even cotton cloth. Jones could not get a bit of
washable cotton anywhere. I had planned to sew
new uniforms for some of our boys. Now I will
have to wait.

Motherhood is glorified in this colonial tapestry showing women's role in support of independence.

Have you any word of our dear friend, **Eliza Lucas Pinckney**? I miss you both so very much. It's hard to have two good neighbors move away.

Word has it that both of Eliza's sons are serving in the war. I pray for their safe return. I can only imagine Mrs. Pinckney's state of mind. She loves those boys so.

With her sons away and her husband dead, she must be running **Belmont** by herself. Can she manage the slaves, do you think? The British stir up so much trouble by hiring the best slaves to serve in their army. But Eliza is so clever! I remember how she overcame so many troubles to get her **indigo** business going.

Do you remember the story? Eliza's father sent her some indigo seeds from the West Indies. She experimented with them for three years until she could get a sturdy plant to grow in our climate.

People and Terms to Know

Eliza Lucas Pinckney—(1722–1793) one of the most important women of colonial America. She developed improved strains of the indigo plant, which became an important source of blue dye. The letters that she wrote about life in colonial times were collected and published in *The Letterbox of Eliza Lucas Pinckney.*

Belmont—plantation overlooking the Cooper River a few miles above Charleston, South Carolina. Eliza Lucas Pinckney inherited Belmont when her husband died.

indigo—blue dye obtained from certain plants. The word is also used for the plant that is used to make the dye. Indigo became an important crop in South Carolina's economy after Eliza Pinckney improved the plant and developed a dye-making business.

She found a way to make blocks of indigo "cakes" to be used for blue dye. The dye became very popular in England. Eliza, along with others, began raising indigo as a cash crop. The money South Carolinians earned from selling the indigo helped the colony survive and prosper during the years before the Revolution.

But who knows what the war has done to Belmont and so many of the other plantations.

But who knows what the war has done to Belmont and so many of the other **plantations**. We hear terrible stories about properties being burned and destroyed. And the slaves . . . I just learned yesterday that Mrs. Watson—you remember her, the old lady in the big white house up the road—why, her slaves robbed her of everything they could carry and then deserted her!

These are times that test the courage of the best of us. Our boys and men are off fighting. We women are left behind to do our best. I have spent days and days tending to the sick and wounded. My home looks more like a hospital than a home.

People and Terms to Know

plantations (plan•TAY•shuhnz)—large estates or farms on which crops are raised and harvested, often by people who live on the plantations.

They bring soldiers to me, some with their legs shattered, others bleeding from the face or stomach. I do the best I can. I wrap their wounds in bandages and feed them what food I can muster. Just this morning, I lost two young men who couldn't have been more than sixteen or seventeen. I thank God that they died peacefully during the night. Pray to God to put a stop to the killing. I feel these deaths as if they were my own sons.

Give my best wishes to your two lovely daughters. And do let me know that you are well. Love to both you and Eliza.

Sarah Doyley

*   *   *

September 25, 1780

My Dear Sarah,

I have just received your letter and rejoice in hearing that you are well. Joy is a feeling my daughters and I have not felt often lately. The war rages on. But we continue as we must.

You asked about our dear friend, Eliza Pinckney. The word is not good. Belmont has been very nearly destroyed. British troops have pulled it to pieces and burned it. Eliza's slaves have deserted her. She has been left alone to survive somehow. Her crops of indigo are very small, since the Negroes deserted during planting and hoeing time.

Within seconds, the soldiers set fire to the big house.

I did not see the British attack on Belmont. But I did see the British destroy the Lark plantation nearby. It was terrible. First, the British soldiers created panic by firing their muskets into the air. Horses, chickens, pigs all ran away in fear. The Lark family and their slaves stayed put inside the big house. Then, within seconds, the soldiers set fire to the big house. The flames could be seen for miles. In fear of death, all inside the house ran for their lives. The British must have taken pity on them. They didn't shoot. Instead, they waited until the plantation was empty. Then they went through the remains, taking wood for their fires and whatever food and medicine they could find.

But the destruction of plantations means little to mothers of sons who are off fighting. A letter just arrived two days ago informing Eliza that her son Thomas has had his leg shattered in the defeat at Camden. Eliza would have gladly parted with her own life, could it have saved her son's leg! She very badly wanted to make the journey to visit him so

▲
Mrs. Schuyler, a Patriot, sets her fields on fire to prevent the approaching British army from getting food.

that she could oversee his care. But smallpox, fever, and flu had broken out among the American prisoners. Thomas insisted that she not expose herself to such deadly diseases. Eliza is very worried about her dear Thomas. I do what I can to comfort her, and she is, after all, a strong and brave woman—so much braver than I.

Mr. Lange and I were never wealthy. But our friend Eliza, as you well know, was so successful with her indigo crops that she had no worries about money. Now the war has changed all that. She cannot pay her bills.

As the Roman poet, **Ovid**, wrote:

> With wavering steps does fickle fortune stray,
>   Nowhere she finds a firm and fixed abode;
> But now all smiles, and now again all frowns,
>   She's constant only in inconstancy.

Lord knows, I don't want to sound bitter. Dear Eliza has been a good and sincere friend, but unlike me, she has enjoyed wealth for many years. Only now, with this dreadful war, has she come to know what it's like to be poor.

Ah, this must be the war talking, not me. Forgive my idle talk. I just can't seem to pull myself together. If it weren't for the girls, I don't know what I'd do.

Yours,
Emily Lange

*   *   *

People and Terms to Know

Ovid—(43 B.C.–A.D. 17) one of the greatest Latin poets, his full name was Publius Ovidius Naso.

Near Charleston, South Carolina
October 13, 1780

M y Dear Emily,

Alas, I have only a few moments to write this note. The British and American troops are much too close. I've been forced to pack whatever I can and leave for my cousin's home, 50 miles away. You can imagine the fear and worry.

I was upset to learn of Eliza's misfortunes. But I worry even more about *your* state of mind. Take heart in knowing that we Patriots are gaining the upper hand. A captain rode by here yesterday and told of a major victory for our side at **King's Mountain**. The end of this terrible war is near. I feel it in my heart. Hold on, my dear friend. Life will be filled with promise soon.

I so look forward to the day when we can all see one another again. The sun will shine brightly. We

---

People and Terms to Know

King's Mountain—rocky ridge near Blackburn, South Carolina, where the Patriots fought a battle on October 7, 1780. All 1,100 men in the British forces were either killed or captured. This victory was the first after a long string of defeats.

will have survived this dreadful war and be the stronger for it.

   With deepest affection,
   Sarah

QUESTIONS TO CONSIDER

1. How did life change for women like Sarah Doyley, Emily Lange, and Eliza Lucas Pinckney during the Revolutionary War?

2. How did Pinckney's experiments with indigo affect the economy of South Carolina?

3. What do the letters tell you about relations between slaves and their masters in South Carolina during the Revolutionary War?

4. Why do you think Emily included the quote from Ovid? What does it mean?

5. How are Sarah and Emily different in the way they react to the war?

READING ON YOUR OWN

Colonial American Home Life
by John F. Warner

Each chapter in this book looks at a different part of colonial life. This book answers questions about how people lived without modern technology. Not only does John F. Warner describe how European settlers lived, but he also writes about the changing lives of Native Americans.

If You Were There in 1776
by Barbara Brenner

What were the lives of children like in 1776? Barbara Brenner shows that the kind of life they led was not the same from colony to colony. Life was also very different for Native American children and children of slaves. This book has wonderful illustrations of colonial times.

Daughter of Liberty:
A True Story of the American Revolution
by Robert M. Quackenbush

Wyn Mabie has just met General George Washington after New York has fallen to the British. Washington needs someone to return to the old army headquarters and retrieve important papers. Wyn volunteers to do the dangerous job, and she quickly learns just how sneaky she has to be to fool the British.

From Confederation
to Constitution

A Little Rebellion

BY BARBARA LITTMAN

Massachusetts, 1786: The Revolutionary War is over. The British government is gone. In its place is a weak alliance, or agreement, of the states under a plan called the **Articles of Confederation**. But there is still unrest in many areas. In western Massachusetts, farmers are going through hard times. The courts are throwing people in jail for not paying their debts. Angry and discouraged, many people have formed into armed bands. They are determined to force a change in government policies.

People and Terms to Know

Massachusetts—one of the 13 British colonies; later a state. The American Revolution began here at the Battles of Lexington and Concord. In 1786, farmers in western Massachusetts revolted against the severe economic conditions that came after the war.

Articles of Confederation—plan for a government of the United States under which the states kept most of the power for themselves. Under the Articles, no president or central leader was called for, and the Congress had no real power.

American artist Howard Pyle (1853–1911) shows Shays planning his rebellion.

"Abigail," said Clarissa Foote in a distracted tone, "I need to go to town. I've brought in the cream for you to churn, and you need to finish spinning that last batch of **flax**. Tomorrow, we'll be pressing the apples, and I want you to help. Your father is working in the south field. But where in the world is Nicholas? Have you seen him?"

"Yes, mother," Abigail replied as she sat down in front of the butter churn. "He took the cows back out to the pasture. Then he said he was going to bring back a basket of apples from the orchard."

"Well, good," Mrs. Foote said with satisfaction. "Tell him to bring in as many baskets as he can. The Grants are coming tomorrow with apples and their cider press. So I want as many apples gathered as possible."

Mrs. Foote took her cloak off its peg by the door and wrapped it around her shoulders. Fall was definitely in the air on this brisk September morning. She stepped outside with mixed emotions. "There is no place on earth more beautiful than these rolling hills of western Massachusetts," she thought. "I wouldn't be anywhere else. I just hope we can survive the winter. If my good husband

---

People and Terms to Know

flax—plant fiber used for making cloth.

Thomas is sent to **debtors' prison** later this year, the children and I will have very hard times."

The Footes lived in the ring of farmhouses closest to the center of town, and Mrs. Foote had always liked the convenient location. Unlike many of the other farm wives, she could walk to town.

She wondered, though, if that cold-hearted Andrew Cane would sell her anything else on credit.

She wanted to serve hearty food tomorrow to her family and guests. Luckily, they had had a good crop of beans this summer. She also still had some salt pork left. The beans were simmering now, and later she would start the corn for the hasty pudding. She wanted something sweet for the children, and to thank the Grants. She wondered, though, if that cold-hearted Andrew Cane would sell her anything else on **credit**.

What can he expect? she asked herself in anger. I can no more pay hard cash for goods than the next

---

People and Terms to Know

debtors' prison—prison where men were sent who could not pay their debts.

credit—trust in a buyer's ability and willingness to pay for goods at a later time.

overtaxed farm wife. But does he support the government issue of **paper money** to help the likes of us? Of course not!

Walking fast now, Mrs. Foote passed the blacksmith shop, the tavern, and the meeting house. Then she reached the general store. As she pulled the door open, she squared her shoulders. She was determined to persuade Mr. Cane to give her credit for a purchase of sugar.

"Morning, Mrs. Foote. It's a beautiful day isn't it? What brings you to town?" asked the storekeeper.

"Good morning to you, too," Mrs. Foote replied. "It's a little sugar I'm needing today."

"Well, that's excellent, excellent," came the response. "And how will you be paying for that today?"

"Now, Mr. Cane, you know I have no cash," Mrs. Foote said with a sigh. "We've talked about this a hundred times. My husband fought for your independence. Then he was handed a **state certificate** in

People and Terms to Know

paper money—money issued by the Continental government after the war, when there was a shortage of coins. Most people considered it worthless.

state certificate—certificate guaranteeing payment to Revolutionary War soldiers for their service in the army.

payment that wasn't worth the paper it was printed on. We've gone from being taxed into the **poorhouse** by the British to being taxed into debtors' prison because of those overpaid politicians in Boston. I'm telling you now, we're not going to take this much longer."

"Well, and what do you propose, Mrs. Foote? I suppose you'd like to see more bands of armed outlaws travelling the countryside disrupting our courts! Is that the solution? As for me, I have a business to run. I can't give my goods away," he replied.

Flushed and angry, Mrs. Foote turned and left the store without another word.

The rest of her day was a flurry of activity. She prepared for the cider pressing the next day. In addition, she and the children had all the regular chores to finish before dark. Ash had been gathered from the fireplace and placed in a large barrel. Water needed to be added and the **lye** collected for making soap. The days were getting shorter now,

---

People and Terms to Know

poorhouse—public home that fed and housed the poor.

lye—potassium carbonate, a strong alkaline substance that results when wood ash is mixed with water. Soap was made by combining lye with liquid animal fat from cooking meat.

and Mrs. Foote wanted Abigail to gather as many bayberries as possible. It might be a luxury, but the sweet smell they added to candles made the long winters more pleasant. She had planned to help Thomas smoke the bees out of the hive the children had found, but that would probably have to wait until after the cider pressing.

The next day dawned crisp and clear, perfect for a cider pressing. The Footes and Grants worked hard all day, making a good supply of cider for both families. After a meal of salt pork, baked beans, hasty pudding, and fresh fruit from the orchard, Mrs. Foote sighed and sat back with satisfaction.

Abigail, Nicholas, and the Grants' two boys were playing jacks with a set of colored stones they had found by the creek. Despite her worries about how the family would make it through the winter, Clarissa was happy. Her mind wandered to all the good times her family and the Grants had shared.

Her daydream was broken, though, by Mr. Grant's loud voice and his fist pounding the table. "Well, I'm going," he said. "Something has to be done to stop the courts from sending good men like us to debtors' prison, Thomas. Just last week, my neighbor was **convicted**, and you'll never find a better, harder-working man. And now he has the legal bills and court fees added to his debt. No one's getting rich here except lawyers and politicians. If those overpaid politicians in the east won't listen, we'll give them something more than talk to think about!"

"No one's getting rich here except lawyers and politicians."

"What is this?" Mrs. Foote asked, turning to her husband.

"Well," he said, "we've heard there's a plan to stop the courts from sending good men to debtors' prison. In spite of all our hopes for the **Hatfield Convention**, nothing's changed. Oh, it's true. We closed the court in August, but now it's business as usual again. They say **Daniel Shays** is leading a group to **Springfield** at the end of the month."

People and Terms to Know

convicted—found guilty in a court of law; in this case, for the crime of not paying money that was owed.

Hatfield Convention—meeting in the town of Hatfield on August 22, 1786, where criticisms of the government were widely publicized.

Daniel Shays—(1747–1825) Revolutionary War captain who led the series of uprisings by farmers of western Massachusetts in 1786 and 1787 that became known as Shays's Rebellion. It called attention to the weakness of the government under the Articles of Confederation and was one of several events that led to the Constitutional Convention.

Springfield—Massachusetts town where Daniel Shays and his followers prevented the court from sitting in September 1786.

"And the two of you are joining him? It scares me. Shays and his followers are frightening. Too many people are demanding that the government do something to stop them. Isn't there a safer way to show the government things need to change?" Mrs. Foote asked.

"Well, dear," came the response. "Talking with the politicians hasn't helped. What other choice do we have? We can't afford to pay the **poll tax**, so we can't change things by voting. Our demands from the Convention have been ignored. What choice does that leave us, but to take action?"

Clarissa sighed and looked at her good friend, Mary Beth Grant. Mary Beth was nodding her head in agreement. With a small nod, and another sigh, Clarissa agreed too.

The days passed quickly. September was a busy month. Corn and beans had to be harvested and set to dry. The wild berries needed gathering, and the last of the fruit from the orchard had to be collected. All this had to be done, of course, in addition to the regular daily chores.

People and Terms to Know

poll tax—tax that men had to pay before they could vote at the polls.

Before Clarissa knew it, the day had come. She had washed and pressed Thomas's Continental Army uniform. Shabby as it had become, he did look handsome standing by his horse with his musket slung over his shoulder. Beckoning him to lean down, she tucked a **hemlock sprig** in the brim of his hat. And then, he was off.

Clarissa, distracted all day, got very little work done. Finally, in the late afternoon, she grabbed her cloak and strode quickly into town. Someone must know what has happened by now, she thought desperately. Just as she rounded the corner past the schoolhouse, she heard the familiar ring of the town crier's bell.

Hurrying toward the sound, she came upon a crowd of people listening anxiously to his report. What? What was this he was saying? Clarissa broke out into a grin. They had stopped the court from meeting. **Governor Bowdoin** had sent more

---

People and Terms to Know

hemlock sprig—small cutting from a hemlock tree (a kind of evergreen). It was a symbol of the people who sided with the rebels during Shays's Rebellion. George Washington had worn hemlock sprigs during the Revolutionary War, and Shays and his men were following that tradition.

Governor Bowdoin—James Bowdoin (1726–1790), American political leader during and after the Revolutionary War, he was the governor of Massachusetts during Shays's Rebellion. He was responsible for stopping the rebellion and helping the states accept the federal Constitution.

than 4,000 soldiers under **General Benjamin Lincoln** to try to defend the courts. But Shays and his men had been able to stop them anyway!

Well, maybe now those politicians will listen, she thought with satisfaction.

Well, maybe now those politicians will listen, she thought with satisfaction. Planning a hearty meal for Thomas's return, Mrs. Foote made her way back to the farmhouse. She hoped this would bring what the farmers of western Massachusetts needed.

*   *   *

Shays's Rebellion was a turning point. Bands of rebels tried to take over other courthouses that fall and winter. On January 25, 1787, Daniel Shays and his followers tried, but failed, to take over the Springfield **Arsenal** again. Even though they failed in that attempt, their rebellion served a purpose. It called attention to a problem that couldn't be solved by the government under the Articles of

People and Terms to Know

General Benjamin Lincoln—(1733–1810) Revolutionary War soldier and secretary of war (1781–1783), he led the Massachusetts soldiers responsible for suppressing Shays's Rebellion.

Arsenal—building used to store weapons and ammunition.

Confederation—people wouldn't accept the government's certificates. A government was needed that was strong enough that people in the different states would believe in it and follow its rules. The government needed money and an army to put down rebellion. So James Madison, Alexander Hamilton, and others proposed a convention to be held in Philadelphia in the spring of 1787. It became the Constitutional Convention.

QUESTIONS TO CONSIDER

1. Why were farmers' wives worried about making it through the winter of 1786 in western Massachusetts?

2. What were three main economic hardships the farmers of western Massachusetts experienced after the Revolutionary War?

3. What reasons did Mr. Grant and Mr. Foote use to justify trying to take the Springfield court by force?

4. Why is the rebellion led by Daniel Shays important in U.S. history?

Shays's Rebellion convinced people that the federal government needed to be stronger. George Washington pointed out that a stronger federal government would help end many problems among the individual states.

The consequences of . . . [an] inefficient government are too obvious to be dwelt upon. Thirteen sovereignties pulling against each other, and all tugging at the federal head, will soon bring ruin upon the whole. . . . let us have [government] by which our lives, liberty, and property will be secured or let us know the worst at once.

Two Days at the Constitutional Convention, 1787

BY DEE MASTERS

Tuesday, June 5th, at quarters in the Indian Queen Inn, Philadelphia

I feel that we are engaged in a great experiment. The eyes of the world are upon us now. Here we sit, delegates from the new states to this **Constitutional Convention**. It is clear that we are not just correcting the Articles of Confederation. We are creating a whole new government. We must try to reach the goals Mr. Jefferson voiced for us in our Declaration

> **People and Terms to Know**
>
> **Constitutional Convention**—(May 1787) meeting in Philadelphia of delegates from the states. The purpose was to reconsider the Articles of Confederation and decide how to make the government work. However, after much discussion, the delegates at the Constitutional Convention agreed to replace the Articles of Confederation with the Constitution that we now have.

George Washington can be seen at the podium at the right in this painting of the Constitutional Convention.

of Independence. It was signed in this very building nine years ago next month.

Our beloved General Washington was voted President of this assembly in the opening session. He said, "Let us raise a standard to which the wise and honest can repair [go]."

Wednesday, June 6th, <u>Committee of the Whole</u>

We are meeting in the East Room of the Philadelphia State House. The blue-gray walls appear cool, but it is terribly hot and humid. To keep out the sun, the blinds are shut upon the high windows on either side. I don't mind the rumble of wagons and clip-clop of horses outside, but all of us are bothered by the flies that swarm in from the nearby stable!

> *The blue-gray walls appear cool, but it is terribly hot and humid.*

On a low platform between two fireplaces sit General Washington's chair and table. They are

---

People and Terms to Know

Committee of the Whole—meeting of all members.

covered with the same green, thick, woolen cloth that covers all the tables.

Directly in front of the President's platform is the table at which **James Madison** has decided to sit. Madison has been very strict and accurate in his note taking. All of us have missed a few meetings, except Madison. I hope he does not hurt his health. He is a small and rather sickly looking man at best.

General Washington has entered. **Mr. Pinckney moves** that the first branch of the National **Legislature** be elected by the State Legislatures, not by the people. His point is that state lawmakers are more fit than the people to judge who would be a good representative. Also, the State Legislatures will have to approve our plan for a new government. They will be more likely to vote for the plan if it gives them a say in choosing the members of that government.

Mr. Rutledge seconds the motion.

People and Terms to Know

James Madison—36-year-old delegate from Virginia. He contributed more ideas to the formation of the Constitution than any other delegate. He would go on to become the fourth president of the United States.

Mr. Pinckney—Charles Pinckney, 29-year-old lawyer and delegate from South Carolina.

moves—in rules for debate: calls for discussion and a vote. The subject being discussed is called the *motion*.

Legislature—government body that makes laws.

Mr. Rutledge—John Rutledge, 47-year-old delegate from South Carolina. He served on the South Carolina Supreme Court.

seconds—in rules for debate: a motion must be seconded, or supported by another person, before it can be debated.

▲

James Madison in 1787.

Mr. Gerry has been recognized to speak. He speaks in favor of Mr. Pinkney's motion. He says he thinks that the people in England will probably lose their liberty because so few have the right to vote. Our danger, he suggests, is that too many may have the right to vote. Why, in Massachusetts, the worst men get into the Legislature. Several members of that body have been convicted lately of serious

People and Terms to Know

Mr. Gerry—43-year-old Elbridge Gerry, signer of the Declaration of Independence and the Articles of Confederation, member of the Continental Congress, and delegate from Massachusetts.

crimes. The British system of nobles and king is evil, but too much democracy has problems too. The people should elect one branch of the government. But the first branch of the legislature should not be chosen directly by the people. Instead, the people should nominate people to this first house and then the State Legislature should select the members from those nominated.

Mr. Wilson disagrees. He argues that the government should be strong. Its strength should come directly from the proper source of all authority, the people. There will be no danger of improper elections if the election districts are large.

Mr. Sherman adds that if we wish to keep State Governments, then we must let them elect the National, or Federal, Government. We should not try to make the Federal Government too powerful. The Federal Government should stick to a few jobs: providing national defense, making treaties with other countries, controlling violent rebellions, and regulating foreign trade.

People and Terms to Know

Mr. Wilson—James Wilson, 44-year-old lawyer and delegate from Pennsylvania.

Mr. Sherman—Roger Sherman, 66-year-old mayor and delegate from Connecticut. He was the only person to sign all four major historic documents: the Declaration of Independence, the Articles of Association, the Articles of Confederation, and the U.S. Constitution.

<u>Colonel Mason</u> suggests that, under our present system, Congress represents the States—not the people of the States. Under the new plan, the *people* will be represented. Therefore, they ought to choose the representatives. There are many problems with democratic governments, but no kind of government is free from faults and evil.

Mr. Madison states that if there is to be a free government, the people must elect at least one branch of the Legislature. With proper controls, he believes that this method gives the people the best representation. It also separates the power of the State Government from that of the Federal Government.

(Mr. Madison is probably the most prepared and informed member of this assembly, but he has a weak voice, and it is always difficult to hear him.)

Mr. Madison continues by noting that Federal Government is needed in order to have some control over large groups. No single group should be large

People and Terms to Know

Colonel Mason—George Mason, 62-year-old planter, delegate from Virginia, and George Washington's neighbor. He wrote most of his state's constitution.

enough to endanger the rights of the **minority**. We have seen what has happened to the rights of the minority in the case of skin color. It has led to the most brutal control ever exercised by man over man. (I wonder how many people realize that Mr. Madison is arguing for a Federal Government so that we may protect the rights of the oppressed African in America?)

He says that the Federal Government will, and should, swallow the State Governments.

Mr. Dickinson suggests that the Senate should be modeled after the House of Lords in the British Government. To help this Senate be separate from State control, representatives should be given longer terms, perhaps seven years.

Mr. Read startles everyone by suggesting that there is too much attention given to State government. He says that the Federal Government will, and should, swallow the State Governments. We should not patch up the old system, he argues. The old system was temporary. If we do not establish a

---

People and Terms to Know

minority—racial, religious, political, or other group regarded as different from the larger group of which it is part.

Mr. Dickinson—John Dickinson, 54-year-old delegate from Delaware. He had been governor of Pennsylvania and was governor of Delaware.

Mr. Read—George Read, 53-year-old lawyer and delegate from Delaware.

good government on new principles, we must either go to ruin or have the work to do over.

Mr. Pierce points out that the new system means the citizens of the States would be represented both as individuals and as a group.

General Pinckney says he wishes to have a good Federal Government and still to leave a large share of the power in the States. But an election of either branch by the people is not practical. People are too scattered in many States, particularly in South Carolina. Legislators chosen by the people will not be any better at preventing bad measures than legislators chosen by State Legislatures. As an example, he tells us that a majority of the people of South Carolina wanted paper money, but the Legislature refused. The Legislature, knowing that paper money is not to be trusted, showed more character and better judgment than the general run of citizens.

Mr. Wilson wished to disagree with Mr. Read's earlier suggestion to do away with State Legislatures. There would be no problem between the two if each had its own job. Nor would the Federal Government

---

People and Terms to Know

Mr. Pierce—William Pierce, 47-year-old businessman and delegate from Georgia.

destroy the States. In history, the opposite was usually true: the parts destroyed the whole.

THE DECISION: Mr. Pinckney's motion—for the State Legislatures to select members of the first branch of the national Government—was defeated eight to three. That leaves the way open for the people to elect their representatives to this first branch directly.

What has surfaced in this debate is the struggle for power, especially between the large and small States. It will not be an easy problem to resolve. Today, though, we must move on to other issues. We have a full schedule. I am sure I will be glad to be back in my room at the Indian Queen Inn tonight.

QUESTIONS TO CONSIDER

1. Why does Mr. Pinckney want the first branch of the National Legislature to be elected by the State Legislatures and not by the people?

2. What is the reason that Mr. Gerry is against letting the people vote for the National Legislature?

3. What is Mr. Mason's argument for letting the people vote for the National Legislature?

4. Why did Mr. Sherman want to keep the Federal Government from being too powerful?

5. What reason did Mr. Madison give for making the Federal Government strong?

6. How would you have voted on Mr. Pinckney's motion if you had been a delegate?

A Kids' Guide to America's Bill of Rights: Curfews, Censorship, and the 100-pound Giant
by Kathleen Krull

This book gives the history of each amendment and discusses legal cases involving children. If you are interested in law, this is a great first reference book.

Shh! We're Writing the Constitution
by Jean Fritz

Did you know that the Constitution was written in a hot, stuffy room that had a bluebottle fly problem? And did you know that the authors shut the windows so that people could not hear what they were saying? All the surprising parts of the Constitutional Convention come alive in this book.

If You Were There When They Signed the Constitution
by Elizabeth Levy

The author gives a lively account of the Constitutional Convention. The format of the book is question-and-answer, and it is cleverly illustrated.

Dear Brother Rat

BY TERRY FIELAND

January 1788

My Dear Brother John,

I want to tell you how much I enjoy your letters, especially our talks about the **Constitution**. Finding the right government for our new country is so important. Even I can see that. Of course, most men think we ladies are too empty-headed to make any sense of the question.

I did hear an interesting discussion at dinner last night. A gentleman from Massachusetts spoke at great length about the Constitution. He took a position that was opposite to everything you believe.

People and Terms to Know

Constitution—Constitution of the United States. The Constitution was signed in Philadelphia on September 17, 1787, and took effect on March 4, 1789.

Alexander Hamilton wrote powerful articles in favor of the Constitution. When the state of New York voted to ratify it (by only 3 votes), a float representing the ship of state honored Hamilton in the victory parade.

More than that, I am now convinced that I must address you as Brother Rat. I suppose that would make Abigail Mrs. Rat. All my nieces and nephews will be the little Rats. You know I am saying this with a smile on my face. Please let me explain.

Everybody is talking about whether to **ratify** the Constitution—whether to create a new government for the country or not. The gentleman at dinner said it was a disagreement between Ratifiers and Anti-Ratifiers, that is, between the Rats and the Anti-Rats. Since you are *for* ratifying the Constitution, you would be one of the Rats. It seemed very funny at the table, and we all had a good laugh.

There was not much laughter after that. The gentleman from Massachusetts went on to frighten us to death with stories of what will happen if the Constitution is adopted. He painted a picture of a federal government that would collect all the power in the hands of a few men. He said it would even do away with the states. There would soon be no more New York or Massachusetts. There would be only one, very large, government. The government

People and Terms to Know

ratify—give official or formal approval or consent. The Constitution had to be ratified, or approved, by specially elected conventions in at least nine of the thirteen states before it would go into effect. Delaware was the first state to ratify it, on December 7, 1787. Rhode Island, the last state to ratify, did so on May 29, 1790.

would be driven to desperate acts in order to control a territory too big to be governed.

You yourself have admitted that most of our fellow New Yorkers do not favor the Constitution. I'm afraid those at dinner were quite in agreement with the gentleman's remarks.

I hope that in the country you find more support for your views on the Constitution than I do in the city.

> *I hope that in the country you find more support for your views on the Constitution than I do in the city.*

Your loving sister,
Mary

*   *   *

February 1788

My Dear Sister Mary,

We Rats are all in fine health. We are warm and snug around the fire these cold winter nights. Abigail is not too pleased to be called Mrs. Rat, but the children think it is great fun. They have spent much time playing at being rats since I read them your letter. It has given me another chance to explain to them why the Constitution must be ratified.

I would rather do that than tell them tales to scare them out of their wits, as your dinner guest seems to have done. I know you have been reading the letters from **Publius** in your newspapers. And I must say, dear sister, that you understand them better than most men that I know. So I suspect you were not all that frightened, after all.

You have my word that the new government under the Constitution will not be the monster that your guest imagined. You might go back and read the five letters from Publius on how the Constitution divides power. By giving different parts of the government some power over the others, the Constitution protects us from the things your dinner guest feared.

It is not that Publius thinks men are angels. (Then again, he has not met you or my dear children, or he might think otherwise.) As Publius said in the last of the five letters, on February 6, if men were angels, no government would be necessary. And if angels were governing men, then no controls on

---

People and Terms to Know

Publius—name under which 85 letters began appearing in New York newspapers in October 1787. They explained the proposed Constitution and argued for its ratification. Alexander Hamilton and James Madison wrote most of the letters. The letters were later published in book form as *The Federalist Papers.* It was not unusual at the time to write about political matters using another name.

government would be necessary. Of course, we are only men, and we will be governed by men under the Constitution.

We have double security, though. The power that the people give to the government is first divided between the states and the federal government. It is divided again, among three departments:

It will not be possible to collect all the power in a few hands.

the **legislative**, the **executive**, and the **judiciary**.

The president cannot become a tyrant because the legislature can **impeach** him. The legislature cannot vote to spend more money than is wise, because the president can **veto** their bills. The judges who serve on federal courts are appointed by the president, and they must be approved by the legislature. With such a separation of powers, it will not be possible to collect all the power in a few hands. If you read Publius's letters again, I think

---

People and Terms to Know

legislative—branch of government that makes laws; Congress. It is made up of the Senate and the House of Representatives.

executive—branch of government responsible for conducting public affairs and executing, or carrying out, the laws of the country. The head of the executive branch is the president.

judiciary—branch of government responsible for interpreting the laws of the country. The Supreme Court heads the judicial system.

impeach—bring a public official before a court on a charge of wrongdoing.

veto—refuse to sign a bill passed by Congress, preventing it from becoming law unless it is passed again by a two-thirds majority in both houses.

you will be convinced that we will be well protected from being oppressed by our government.

Publius says it better than I. Read his words until I write again.

John, your Brother Rat

*   *   *

May 1788

My Dear Sister Mary,

New York will finally have a Convention to decide whether to ratify the Constitution or not. I voted last Tuesday for delegates to the Convention. Delaware, Pennsylvania, New Jersey, Georgia,

UNITED THEY STAND—DIVIDED FALL.

▲

A cartoon shows the strength the states gain by ratifying the Constitution.

Connecticut, and Massachusetts have already ratified the Constitution. Here we sit in New York,
only now choosing our Convention delegates. The
New York Convention will not even meet until the
middle of June. Who knows what other states will
have ratified by then. How frustrated I am to be
among the last!

I comfort myself by thinking perhaps it is just as
well that other states go before us. If the vote were
taken today, I don't believe the New York delegates
would approve it. New York has done well enough
under the Articles of Confederation. Many are
afraid that under a new government we will have
to give up many liberties and advantages.

Spring is a busy time here on the farm, but I
promise to write again soon.

John, your Brother Rat

* * *

July 1788

M y Dear Brother Rat,

Cheers! The Rats have won. Even New York has
now ratified the Constitution. We have a new government. I am so happy. I am also pleased that
George Washington will certainly have a role in it. He

seems to make people feel so much better, even those who still have questions about the Constitution.

Please find a few minutes to write. Give my love to Abigail and the little Rats.

Your loving sister,
Mary

*　　*　　*

August 1788

My Dear Sister Mary,

I hope that the recent hot weather has not been too unpleasant. You sound as happy as I am that the Constitution has been ratified. The New York Convention held out to the end. I believe the delegates were still not in favor of ratification. New Hampshire forced them into it.

When New Hampshire ratified, that made nine states. Of course, nine states were all that were required for the Constitution to be adopted. New York could not stop the Constitution from going into effect. Our only choice was to ratify and remain part of the Union or refuse and make our way on our own. In the end, New York made the right decision.

I share your feelings about George Washington. We are blessed to have him amongst us. It is my hope that he will be our first president. We live in exciting times. We have witnessed the creation of a government the likes of which the world has never seen. And I have so enjoyed being able to share it with you in our letters.

Your loving brother,
John, a proud Rat

QUESTIONS TO CONSIDER

1. What did Publius mean by the statement, "If men were angels, no government would be necessary"?

2. How did the Constitution protect the people from a few men gaining power?

3. How many states had to ratify the Constitution for it to be adopted?

4. Why did New York finally ratify the Constitution?

Benjamin Banneker Surveys the New Capital

BY JUDITH LLOYD YERO

Finally! Our class had planned this trip to Washington, D.C., all year. The bus trip was a drag—a lot of sitting—but it was worth it. At last we were seeing all the places we'd learned about. Now we were standing in line waiting to get into the Washington Monument. Our teacher, Mr. Cooper, asked if anyone had questions about what we'd seen so far.

"If the First Continental Congress met in Philadelphia, how come they didn't build the capital there?"

"Good question, Alicia," Mr. Cooper said. "It wasn't an easy decision. By the time the colonies won independence, the people were very proud of what they'd done. They wanted to show the world that this was a great nation, but the new United States of

Benjamin Banneker in 1791.

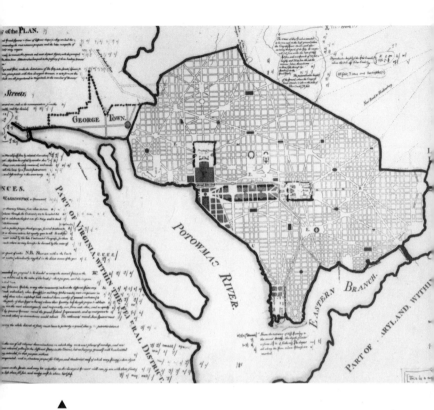

▲

The original plan of Washington, D.C. in 1790.

America didn't even have a capital. People from different cities began to argue about where it should be.

"Philadelphians obviously thought the capital should be there. Boston argued that because they fired the first shots of the Revolution, Boston should be the capital. Yorktown disagreed. That's where the last shot was fired and where, they claimed, independence had been won. No one could agree.

"In 1789, New York became a front-runner. The new Congress was to meet there to **inaugurate** George Washington as the first president. New York spent lots of money fixing up their city hall. They put in marble walls and floors and built impressive statues. Visitors said it was the most beautiful building they'd ever seen. That's just what the New Yorkers wanted. But members of Congress from other states said it was just a cheap trick.

"They would build the capital at the center of the thirteen colonies."

"To make peace, Secretary of State Thomas Jefferson suggested they build a new city as the capital. There was very little money in the treasury, but the people liked the idea. They would build the capital at the center of the thirteen colonies. Land in Maryland and Virginia would be used, but the capital city, Washington, would stand in a separate district—the District of Columbia.

"Well, when word got out, President Washington got a letter from a young Frenchman,

People and Terms to Know

inaugurate (ihn•AH•gyoo•rayt)—swear into office. An *inauguration* is a formal ceremony during which the elected official, before officially taking over the office, promises to serve the people.

Major Pierre L'Enfant, who had fought with the Continental Army. L'Enfant was an engineer, and he asked Washington if he could design the new city. He admitted that he wanted to do it to make a name for himself. Washington knew L'Enfant from the war, and he liked him. He agreed, but many people didn't like the idea of a 'foreigner' designing the capital of their nation. "

The line at the monument was moving very slowly, and some of us were getting a little fidgety. "Okay, class," said Mr. Cooper. "Here's a riddle for you. What do a pail of milk, an African prince, caterpillars, a clock, and stars have to do with Washington, D.C.?"

Mr. Cooper loved to give us riddles to solve. He was really trying to keep us from getting antsy from standing in line. But he knew some great stories that weren't in our history books, so we played along.

"Back in the 1600s, an English milkmaid named Molly Walsh was accused of stealing a pail of milk. She was sent to Maryland as punishment. When

---

People and Terms to Know

Major Pierre L'Enfant (lahn•FAHNT)—Major Pierre-Charles L'Enfant (1754–1825), French-born American engineer, architect, and designer who drew up the first plans for Washington, D.C., in 1791.

her punishment was over, Molly bought a farm and two slaves to help her work it. When the farm became successful, she freed the slaves. Later, she married one of her former slaves. He was an African prince who'd been captured and shipped to America. His name was Banna Ka, but the family was known by the name of Bannecky.

"When their grandson, **Benjamin**, was very young, Molly taught him to read and count. Even when he was little, Benjamin loved numbers. He counted everything—the weeds he pulled from the ground and even the caterpillars he picked off the tobacco plants. When Benjamin finally went to school, the teacher wrote his last name as Banneker. Benjamin liked school because there he got to read all the books he wanted.

"Everyone liked Benjamin. He was polite and he had a quick mind. One man, noticing young Benjamin's interest in his watch, lent it to the boy to study. Benjamin carefully took the back off the watch and drew pictures of all the gears and other tiny parts. Over the next two years, he spent every free moment carving gears from wood to build a

---

People and Terms to Know

Benjamin—Benjamin Banneker (1731–1806), self-educated mathematician, astronomer, compiler of almanacs, inventor, and writer. He was one of the first important black American thinkers. Scientists in this and other countries respected him for his knowledge of mathematics and astronomy.

clock that chimed every hour. The clock he built ran perfectly for forty years. It became famous as the first clock built in the New World."

"Benjamin had the ability to do just about anything he wanted."

The line edged closer to the entrance of the Washington Monument. We were all eager to get inside and start climbing. But we also wanted to hear the end of Mr. C.'s story.

"Benjamin had the ability to do just about anything he wanted. But when his father died, he inherited the farm and had to spend all of his days working the land. He did this for many years, but he never gave up his love of numbers. One night, when he was in his fifties, Benjamin started studying the stars. Every night, after a long day in the fields, he would draw pictures of the constellations and the paths of the planets. He got so good, he could predict an eclipse.

"In those days, farmers bought a book called an **almanac** every year. The almanac contained

---

People and Terms to Know

almanac (AHL•muh•nak)—calendar-like book with astronomical information, weather forecasts, and other useful information. For many years, Benjamin Franklin published an almanac called *Poor Richard's Almanac*.

▲

Mounted on a tripod, this surveying instrument (called a *transit*) was one used by Benjamin Banneker in surveying the District of Columbia.

weather forecasts, information about the movement of the stars, and lots of charts and tables on just about anything. Farmers depended on their almanacs to decide when to plant and harvest their crops. Benjamin decided he could write his own almanac—so he did. But no one wanted to publish it because they didn't believe that a black man could know enough to write such a complicated book."

"Hey, Mr. C., we know how the cow, the prince, the caterpillars, the clock, and the stars fit together," asked Alicia, "but what did Benjamin have to do with Washington?"

"After Major L'Enfant was hired to design the capital city, Thomas Jefferson asked **Major Andrew Ellicott**, a **surveyor**, to map and survey the area where the city would be built. Because he was Benjamin's neighbor, Ellicott knew how smart Benjamin was in mathematics and astronomy. He asked Benjamin to work with him. At first, people thought Benjamin was the major's servant, but they soon learned that he knew more than any of them about surveying.

"Many people wanted to get in on the act and build on the land around the new capital. They knew they could make a lot of money when it was finished. But L'Enfant wouldn't let people see the

---

People and Terms to Know

Major Andrew Ellicott—(1754–1820) best known surveyor of his day, he conducted many surveys to establish state and territorial boundaries. He mapped the Mississippi River and encouraged Congress to purchase the Louisiana Territory as a way to expand the territory of the United States.

surveyor (sihr•VAY•uhr)—person who uses mathematics to locate land boundaries and determine where to place buildings or other structures on a piece of land. A *survey* of a piece of land tells the owner exactly where the land is in terms of latitude and longitude.

Banneker used this compass to survey the District of Columbia.

map and his plans. No one could figure out exactly where the best place to build would be. Of course, the surveyor had to see the plans, so Benjamin spent a lot of time studying them.

"One day, after many fights with the men who were in charge of the project, L'Enfant stormed off the job and took his plans with him. Everyone thought they'd have to start all over because there weren't any other copies. But Benjamin Banneker saved the day. He told Jefferson that he could redraw the plans of the city—and he did. Construction of the capital went on as scheduled."

At last, we were inside the monument and had climbed to the top. As we looked out through the windows, I had to wonder how different Washington might look if Benjamin Banneker hadn't had such a good memory.

QUESTIONS TO CONSIDER

1. Why did Thomas Jefferson suggest that the United States build a new city for the nation's capital?

2. How did Benjamin show people that he was more than Major Ellicott's servant?

3. How do you think Benjamin gained the respect of many people in a time when slavery was common?

4. What do you think might have happened if Benjamin hadn't been able to redraw the plans for the nation's capital?

Benjamin Banneker: Astronomer and Mathematician
by Laura Baskes Litwin

Benjamin Banneker not only worked on the plan for Washington, D.C.—he was also a farmer, astronomer, mathematician, and writer. He spoke out against racism and was a part of the early abolitionist movement. This illustrated biography gives a clear description of Banneker's life.

Adventure Tales of Benjamin Banneker
by Jody Potts

This book is very different from most history books. It describes Benjamin Banneker's life in both a right-brain (artistic, creative) and left-brain (scientific, orderly) format. Benjamin Banneker was creative and brilliant, and this book captures his life in its own creative way.

Benjamin Banneker: Journey to Freedom
by Melissa Maupin

Stories from Benjamin Banneker's childhood help to explain how he became so successful in so many professions.

Sources

Patrick Henry Protests the Stamp Act *by Danny Miller*

This is a fictional newspaper account based on real events in the House of Burgesses in May 1765. After the debate on Patrick Henry's resolutions, the British governor of Virginia shut down the House of Burgesses. However, the colonists' resistance to the Stamp Act was eventually successful. The Act was repealed by Parliament in March 1766. Ten years after his Stamp Act speech, while urging Virginians to take arms to defend themselves, Patrick Henry spoke his most famous line: "I know not what course others may take; but as for me, give me liberty or give me death." For more information on this great American, see the two-volume set *Patrick Henry: Patriot in the Making* and *Patrick Henry: Practical Revolutionary* by Robert Douthat Meade (Philadelphia and New York: J.B. Lippincott Company, 1957, 1969).

The Daughters of Liberty Stage a Boycott
by Judith Lloyd Yero

The letter writers in this story are fictional. Mercy Otis Warren, Samuel Adams, and the Daughters of Liberty were historical figures. The poem in the *Pennsylvania Gazette* was actually published in 1768, but the author was anonymous. She was believed to be a Quaker lady who lived in Philadelphia and was a member of the Daughters of Liberty. A book that gives insights into the people of the time during and preceding the American Revolution is *Cast for a Revolution: Some American Friends and Enemies,* by Jean Fritz (Boston: Houghton Mifflin, 1972).

Trouble in Boston *by Terry Fieland*

The narrator and his son, Quincy, are fictional. The other people and events are real. Two opposing accounts of the Boston Massacre can be found on the web site, www.ukans.edu: "Anonymous Account of the Boston Massacre," University of Gronigen; and "Captain Thomas Preston's Account of the Boston Massacre, 13 March, 1770," Account from the British Public Records Office.

The Boston Tea Party *by Mary Kathleen Flynn*

The letter writer Anne and her family are fictional characters, but Samuel Adams, King George, Governor Hutchinson and Admiral Montague were all historical figures. The story is based on *The Oxford Companion to United States History* (Oxford New York: Oxford University Press, 2001), the Boston Tea Party Ship and Museum web site (www.bostonteapartyship.com), and an eyewitness account written by George Hewes (www.historyplace.com). Additional facts come from The British Monarchy: The Official Web Site (www.royal.gov.uk) and The East India Company web site (www.theeastindiacompany.com).

Common Sense **Changes Minds** *by Stephen Currie*

John and Elizabeth Hastings are fictional characters. The details of their home life are historical. The points of view they express about the worsening situation between the colonies and England are similar to many held by colonists at the time of this story. The phrases they quote from Thomas Paine's *Common Sense* can be found in *Rights of Man, Common Sense, and other Political Writings* by Thomas Paine (Oxford; New York: Oxford University Press, 1995). Historian Bernard Bailyn provides an analysis of how Paine's writing moved so many people's opinions in "Thomas Paine" in *Faces of Revolution* (New York: Alfred A. Knopf, Inc., 1990).

The Battle of Saratoga *by Walter Hazen*

Caleb, Mr. Dandridge, and Captain Morris are fictional characters. All other persons mentioned in the story are historical figures. Complete and accurate books that contain more information on the famous battle include: *The Battle of Saratoga,* by Rupert Furneaux (New York: Stein and Day, 1971) and *Saratoga,* by David C. King (Brookfield, CT: Twenty-First Century Books, 1998).

Valley Forge *by Brian J. Mahoney*

This story is a fictional account based on excerpts from the diary of surgeon Albigence Waldo, and various accounts of Valley Forge. George Washington struggled to keep the American Army together in the face of embarrassing defeats, low supplies, low morale, and questionable popular and political support. The half-starved, sickly army that camped at Valley Forge through the winter of 1778 emerged in June as the professional fighting force that would ultimately defeat the British at Yorktown. You can learn more about Valley Forge online at http://www.ushistory.org/valleyforge/index.html. Books about Valley Forge include *Ordeal at Valley Forge* (Philadelphia, PA: University of Pennsylvania Press, 1963) and *Valley Forge, The Making of an Army* (New York: Harper & Brothers, 1952).

The *Bonhomme Richard* Fights the *Serapis*
by Diane Wilde

John Paul Jones's story reads almost like a legend, but the story is historically accurate. Captain Landais and Captain Pearson, along with all the others involved in the story, are historical figures. John Paul Jones wrote a full report of the battle that can be read at the website of the John Paul Jones Cottage Museum, Scotland, www.jpj.demon.co.uk/jpjflamb.htm.

The Swamp Fox *by Judith Conaway*

These words by Mary Esther Videau are imaginary. So are the descriptions of what she was doing during the American Revolution and of how she "conquered" General Marion. But Mary Esther Videau Marion was a real person. The few things we know about her come from early accounts of General Marion's life. Sources for this story include *Rebels and Redcoats, The American Revolution Through the Eyes of Those Who Fought and Lived It* by George F. Scheer and Hugh F. Rankin (New York: Da Capro Press, 1988), and *The Life of Francis Marion*, by W. Gilmore Simms (Stratford, NH: Ayer Company Publishers).

Life on the Home Front *by Jane Leder*

The two letter writers, Sarah Doyley and Emily Lange, are fictional characters. Eliza Lucas Pinckney, Thomas Pinckney, and General Howe are all historical figures. The major sources for information about these people were "Letters of Eliza Lucas Pinckney, 1768–1782," (*The South Carolina Historical Magazine*, vol. 76, no. 3, July 1975) and Dr. Frank Clark's "The Revolutionary War," www.foclark.tripod.com.

A Little Rebellion *by Barbara Littman*

The characters in this story are fictional, but the details of their lives give an accurate picture of the activities, problems, and opinions of many in western Massachusetts who were sympathetic to Daniel Shays. Sources include *Western Massachusetts in the Revolution* by Robert J. Taylor (Providence, RI: Brown University Press, 1954) and *Shays' Rebellion: The Making of an Agrarian Insurrection* by David P. Szatmary (Amherst: University of Massachusetts Press, 1980).

Two Days at the Constitutional Convention, 1787
by Dee Masters

The narrator of this story is a fictional delegate to the Constitutional Convention, but all the information about the delegates is accurate. We know about the details of this historic meeting from the many letters and journal entries the delegates themselves wrote. A good summary is provided in historian Fred Barbash's *The Founding* (New York: Simon & Schuster, 1987.) The debates themselves can be read in *Documents Illustrative of the Formation of the American States* arranged by Charles C. Tansill (U.S. Government Printing Office, 1927).

Dear Brother Rat *by Terry Fieland*

The letters between Mary and John are fictional, and so are the characters who wrote them. The information they present about the debate going on over ratification of the Constitution is accurate. Sources include *Witnesses at the Creation: Hamilton, Madison, Jay, and the Constitution* by Richard B. Morris (New York: Holt, Rinehart, and Winston, 1985) and *Birth of the Constitution* by Edmund Lindop (Hillside, NJ: Enslow Publishers, Inc., 1987).

Benjamin Banneker Surveys the New Capital
by Judith Lloyd Yero

The narrator, his classmates, and Mr. Cooper are fictional. All other people and events are historically accurate. Benjamin's achievements as an inventor, mathematician, astronomer, and writer are recorded in letters from the publisher of his almanacs, letters written to him by Thomas Jefferson, and his own papers. He was the first black man to receive a presidential appointment to a government position—surveyor of Washington, D.C. A good source of information on the life of Benjamin Banneker is *Your Most Humble Servant* by Shirley Graham (New York: Julian Messner, 1969).

Glossary of People and Terms to Know

Adams, John—(1735–1826) American Patriot and the second president of the United States. John Adams and Samuel Adams were cousins.

Adams, Samuel—(1722–1803) leader of Boston protests against the British and a signer of the Declaration of Independence.

alienate—set aside.

almanac (AL•muh•nak)—calendar-like book with astronomical information, weather forecasts, and other useful information. For many years, Benjamin Franklin published an almanac called *Poor Richard's Almanac.*

Arnold, Benedict—(1741–1801) American major general who played a leading role in the Battle of Saratoga. He later turned traitor and fought for the British.

arsenal—building used to store weapons and ammunition.

Articles of Confederation—plan for a government of the United States under which the states kept most of the power for themselves. Under the Articles, no president or central leader was called for, and the Congress had no real power.

Attucks, Crispus—(c. 1723–1770) Little is known about his life before the night of the Boston Massacre. Most historians say he was black. He may have been a runaway slave, and he may have been a sailor. He is the best-remembered victim of the Boston Massacre, and a monument in his honor stands in the Boston Common.

Banneker, Benjamin—(1731–1806) self-educated mathematician, astronomer, compiler of almanacs, inventor, and writer. He was one of the first important black American thinkers. Scientists in this and other countries respected him for his knowledge of mathematics and astronomy.

Belmont—plantation overlooking the Cooper River a few miles above Charleston, South Carolina. Eliza Lucas Pinckney inherited Belmont when her husband died.

Bonhomme Richard—battleship commanded by John Paul Jones. The ship was given to Jones by the French king and named in honor of Benjamin Franklin, author of *Poor Richard's Almanac.*

Boston Tea Party—event on the evening of December 16, 1773, when the people of Boston threw chests of tea overboard to protest against Great Britain.

bow—front section of a ship or boat.

Bowdoin, James—(1726–1790), American political leader during and after the Revolutionary War, he was the governor of Massachusetts during Shays's Rebellion. He was responsible for stopping the rebellion and helping the states accept the federal Constitution.

boycott—refusal of a group to buy or provide goods or services. The word *boycott* was first used in the 1880s, when laborers in County Mayo, Ireland, refused to work for Captain Boycott, the agent of an English landowner.

broadside—shooting of all the guns on one side of a ship at the same time.

Bunker Hill—Battle of Bunker Hill. It was fought near Boston in June 1775. The British won, but they had 1,054 casualties. The Patriots had 450.

burgess—member of Virginia's colonial legislature.

Burgoyne, General (John)—(1722–1792) British officer whose defeat at the Battle of Saratoga was the turning point of the war. He was called "Gentleman Johnny" because he was a member of fashionable society, a politician, and a playwright in addition to being a soldier.

Camden—town in north-central South Carolina that was the site of a major British victory in the American Revolution.

caper—wild prank.

cargo—goods carried by a ship or other vehicle.

Charleston—port city that is the capital of South Carolina. At the time of the American Revolution, it was the fourth largest city in the colonies, after Philadelphia, New York, and Boston.

civilians—people not in the military.

Committee of the Whole—meeting of all members.

Common Sense—famous pamphlet that persuaded many Americans a complete break with England was necessary. It was written by Thomas Paine and published in January 1776.

Constitutional Convention—(May 1787) meeting in Philadelphia of delegates from the states. The purpose was to reconsider the Articles of Confederation and decide how to make the government work. However, after much discussions, the delegates at the Constitutional Convention agreed to replace the Articles of Confederation with the Constitution that we now have.

Constitution—Constitution of the United States. The Constitution was signed in Philadelphia on September 17, 1787, and took effect on March 4, 1789.

Continental—Money issued by the Continental Congress in 1775 to fund the war. Citizens lost confidence as more money was printed than Congress could actually back up with gold and silver. If Britain won the war, the Continental currency would be worthless, and people often refused to accept it.

Continental Congress—group of men who officially represented and acted for the various colonies, first in 1774 (First Continental Congress), and later 1775–1781 (Second Continental Congress).

Continentals—soldiers who served in the Continental Army, fighting for American independence.

convicted—found guilty in a court of law.

convoy—group of ships moving together with one or more escort ships for protection.

Cornwallis, General Charles—(1738–1805) British general who led the army in the South and surrendered to the Americans at Yorktown.

credit—trust in a buyer's ability and willingness to pay for goods at a later time.

Custom House—building where taxes on goods coming into the colonies were paid to the British.

Daughters of Liberty—organization of women who supported the boycott of British goods. Instead of buying items made in England, the women made their own.

debtors' prison—prison where men were sent who could not pay their debts.

Dickinson, John—(1732–1808) 54-year-old Constitutional Convention delegate from Delaware. He had been governor of Pennsylvania and was governor of Delaware.

East India Company—world's largest trading company at one time.

Ellicott, Andrew—(1754–1820) best known surveyor of his day, he conducted many surveys to establish state and territorial boundaries. He mapped the Mississippi River and encouraged Congress to purchase the Louisiana Territory as a way to expand the territory of the United States.

executive—branch of government responsible for conducting public affairs and executing, or carrying out, the laws of the country. The head of the executive branch is the president.

fife—small flute.

firecake—small bread or roll made of meal and water and cooked over an open fire.

flax—plant fiber used for making cloth.

forage—search for food.

Franklin, Benjamin—(1706–1790) American statesman, author, and scientist.

French—government of France. The French tried to gain control of North America in the 1750s. In 1763, they were defeated by the English and the American colonists in the French and Indian war.

French and Indian War—(1754–1763) conflict in which American colonists and British soldiers battled the French and their Indian allies over which European power would control most of North America.

Gates, General Horatio—(1727–1808) American commander at the Battle of Saratoga in New York.

George III—king of England from 1760 until 1820 during the time when the American colonies gained independence from England.

Gerry, Elbridge—(1744–1814) 43-year-old signer of the Declaration of Independence and the Articles of Confederation, member of the Continental Congress, and delegate to the Constitutional Convention from Massachusetts.

grappling irons—iron claws on the ends of ropes used to fasten an enemy ship alongside before boarding.

greenwood—freshly cut damp wood that creates a lot of smoke as it burns.

Grenville, George—(1712–1770) English politician who made the colonists angry by supporting the Stamp Act and the Townshend Acts.

grog—drink of rum diluted with water.

Hatfield Convention—meeting in the town of Hatfield on August 22, 1786, where criticisms of the government were widely publicized.

hemlock sprig—small cutting from a hemlock tree (a kind of evergreen). It was a symbol of the people who sided with the rebels during Shays's Rebellion. George Washington had worn hemlock sprigs during the Revolutionary War, and Shays and his men were following that tradition.

Henry, Patrick—(1736–1799) American lawyer, Patriot, and public speaker.

Hessians—soldiers from Germany hired by the British to fight against the Americans in the Revolutionary War.

Homer—Greek poet and author of two famous long poems, the *Iliad* and the *Odyssey*, written around 750 B.C.

homespun—rough cloth made of yarn spun at home. All social classes wore clothing made of homespun during the boycott of British goods.

House of Burgesses—law-making branch of colonial Virginia's government.

Howe, Sir William—(1729–1814) Commander-in-Chief of British forces in America from 1776 to 1778.

Huguenot (HYOO•guh•noh)— French protestant. Many Huguenots left France to escape religious persecution. They were among the first European settlers of South Carolina.

Hutchinson, Thomas— (1711–1780) governor of the Massachusetts Colony at the time of the Boston Massacre. The governor was appointed by the British.

impeach—bring a public official before a court on a charge of wrongdoing.

inaugurate (ihn•AH•gyoo•rayt)— swear into office. An *inauguration* is a formal ceremony during which the elected official, before officially taking over the office, promises to serve the people.

indigo—blue dye obtained from certain plants. The word is also used for the plant that is used to make the dye. Indigo became an important crop in South Carolina's economy after Eliza Pinckney improved the plant and developed a dye-making process.

Jefferson, Thomas—(1743–1826) American statesman who became third President of the United States (1801–1809).

Jones, John Paul—(1747–1792) naval captain of the American Revolution. His famous battle cry, "I have not yet begun to fight," is carved above his tomb.

judiciary—branch of government responsible for interpreting the laws of the country. The Supreme Court heads the judicial system.

King's Mountain—rocky ridge near Blackburn, South Carolina, where the Patriots fought a battle on October 7, 1780. All 1,100 men in the British forces were either killed or captured. This victory was the first after a long string of defeats.

L'Enfant, Major Pierre-Charles (lahn•FAHNT)—(1754–1825) French-born American engineer, architect, and designer who drew up the first plans for Washington, D.C., in 1791.

legislative—branch of government that makes laws; Congress. It is made up of the Senate and the House of Representatives.

legislature—government body that makes laws.

Lexington—Battles of Lexington and Concord, on April 19, 1775, marked the beginning of the Revolutionary War. The battle started when 70 Patriots challenged a British patrol on its way to Concord to seize the rebels' military supplies. Eight colonists died, and ten were wounded.

Lincoln, Benjamin—(1733–1810) Revolutionary War soldier and secretary of war (1781–1783), he led the Massachusetts soldiers responsible for suppressing Shays's Rebellion.

Loyalist—American colonist who remained loyal to King George and opposed independence from Great Britain.

lye—potassium carbonate, a strong alkaline substance that results when wood ash is mixed with water. Soap was made by combining lye with liquid animal fat from cooking meat.

Madison, James—(1751–1826) 36-year-old Constitutional Convention delegate from Virginia. He contributed more ideas to the formation of the Constitution than any other delegate. He would go on to become the fourth president of the United States.

mainmast—tallest mast of a sailing ship; a heavy pole that holds up the largest sail.

Marion, Francis—(c. 1732–1795) American revolutionary commander known as the Swamp Fox. In 1780, he led a small force of men against the British in South Carolina. They staged surprise attacks, cut British supply lines, and rescued American prisoners. After the war, Marion was elected to the senate of South Carolina.

Mason, George—(1725–1792) 62-year-old planter, Constitutional Convention delegate from Virginia, and George Washington's neighbor. He wrote most of his state's constitution.

Massachusetts—one of the 13 British Colonies; later a state. The American Revolution began here at the Battles of Lexington and Concord. In 1786, farmers in western Massachusetts revolted against the severe economic conditions that came after the war.

Maverick, Samuel—one of the five people killed in the Boston Massacre. He was seventeen. Three of the eleven who were killed or wounded were reported to be the same age.

minority—racial, religious, political, or other group regarded as different from the larger group of which it is a part.

moves—in rules for debate: calls for discussion and a vote. The subject being discussed is called the *motion*.

musket—shoulder gun used from the 1500s through the 1700s.

mutton—meat from a full-grown sheep.

Navigation Acts—series of laws passed by Parliament to control trade between England and its colonies.

North Sea—body of water that stretches north from the English Channel to the Norwegian Sea. It falls between the east coast of England and the west coasts of Belgium, The Netherlands, Germany, and Denmark.

Ovid—(43 B.C.–A.D. 17) one of the great Latin poets, his full name was Publius Ovidius Naso.

Paine, Thomas—(1737–1809) Englishman who immigrated to America before the Revolution. He was the author of *Common Sense*.

paper money—issued by the Continental government after the war, when there was a shortage of coins. Most people considered it worthless.

Parliament—legislative (law making) branch of government in Great Britain. It includes the House of Lords and the House of Commons.

Patriot—member of the group of colonists who thought the colonies should be a country independent from Britain. Only about one-third of all colonists were Patriots.

petitions—formal requests for rights or benefits from an authority.

Philadelphia—city in Pennsylvania that was the nation's capital before Washington, D.C. The Continental Congress met in Philadelphia.

Pierce, William—47-year-old businessman and Constitutional Convention delegate from Georgia.

Pinckney, Charles—(1746–1825) 29-year-old lawyer and Constitutional Convention delegate from South Carolina.

Pinckney, Eliza Lucas—(1722–1793) one of the most important women of colonial America. She developed improved strains of the indigo plant, which became an important source of blue dye. The letters that she wrote about life in colonial times were collected and published in *The Letterbox of Eliza Lucas Pinckney*.

plantations—(plan•TAY•shuhnz) large estates or farms on which crops are raised and harvested, often by people who live on the plantations.

poorhouse—public home that fed and housed the poor.

poll tax—tax men had to pay before they could vote at the polls.

Preston, Captain Thomas—officer in charge of the British troops at the Boston Massacre. He was charged with murder but found "not guilty" in the trial that followed.

Publius—name under which 85 letters began appearing in New York newspapers in October 1787. They explained the proposed Constitution and argued for its ratification. Alexander Hamilton and James Madison wrote most of the letters. The letters were later published in book form as *The Federalist Papers*. It was not unusual at the time to write about political matters using another name.

quartermaster—person who oversees army supplies.

ratify—give official or formal approval or consent. The Constitution had to be ratified, or approved, by specially elected conventions in at least nine of the thirteen states before it would go into effect. Delaware was the first state to ratify it, on December 7, 1787. Rhode Island, the last state to ratify, did so on May 29, 1790.

Read, George—(1733–1808) 53-year-old lawyer and Constitutional Convention delegate from Delaware.

repeal—cancel officially; undo.

Revere, Paul—(1735–1818) gifted engraver and silversmith. He is best remembered for his ride on April 18, 1775, warning the colonists that the British troops were coming.

Rutledge, John—(1739–1800) 47-year-old Constitutional Convention delegate from South Carolina. He served on the South Carolina Supreme Court.

seconds—in rules for debate: a motion must be seconded, or supported by another person, before it can be debated.

Serapis (suh•RAY•pihs)—British warship. It had three masts, square-rigged sails, and a row of guns along the length of its decks.

Shays, Daniel—(1747–1825) Revolutionary War captain who led the series of uprisings by farmers of western Massachusetts in 1786 and 1787 that became known as Shays's Rebellion. It called attention to the weakness of the government under the Articles of Confederation and was one of several events that led to the Constitutional Convention.

Sherman, Roger—(1721–1793) 66-year-old mayor and Constitutional Convention delegate from Connecticut. He was the only person to sign all four major historic documents: the Declaration of Independence, the Articles of Association, the Articles of Confederation, and the U.S. Constitution.

skirmish—short fight between small groups of soldiers.

Spanish—government of Spain. At the time of the American Revolution, Florida and much of the land west of the Mississippi River belonged to Spain.

spinning bees—gatherings at which women spun wool into yarn for making clothing.

Springfield—Massachusetts town where Daniel Shays and his followers prevented the court from sitting in September 1786.

Stamp Act—law passed by British Parliament in March 1765 requiring American colonists to buy a tax stamp for all printed materials.

state certificate—certificate guaranteeing payment to Revolutionary War soldiers for their service in the army.

stern—rear section of a ship or boat.

Steuben, Baron von—(1730–1794) German general who helped turn George Washington's army into a well-trained fighting force.

struck—pulled down its flag; that is, surrendered.

surplus—more than is needed; excess.

surveyor (sihr•VAY•uhr)—person who uses mathematics to locate land boundaries and determine where to place buildings or other structures on a piece of land. A *survey* of a piece of land tells the owner exactly where the land is in terms of latitude and longitude.

tactic—plan of action.

Tarleton, Sir Banastre—(1754–1833) British officer during the American Revolution known for his cruelty. He was especially hated by the Patriots of South Carolina.

Tories—Loyalists, colonists who supported continued rule by Great Britain. *Tory* comes from an Irish slang word meaning "robber" or "outlaw." Like the Patriots, Tories were against taxation without representation, but they feared the violence and disorder that could result from overturning the government.

Townshend Acts—(1767) series of British laws putting taxes on such imported products as tea, paint, paper, and glass sold in the American colonies. The Acts were made to replace the income lost when the Stamp Act was repealed.

treason—high crime of betrayal of or disloyalty to one's country.

tyranny—unchecked power.

Union Jack—nickname for the British flag.

veto—refuse to sign a bill passed by Congress, preventing it from becoming law unless it is passed again by a two-thirds majority in both houses.

voluntarily—of one's own free will.

Waldo, Albigence—(1750–1794) surgeon at Valley Forge whose diary contained detailed accounts of the army's sufferings.

War for Independence—name for the American Revolution (1775–1783) used by writers of the time.

Warren, Mercy Otis—(1728–1814) writer and poet who, with her brother, James Otis, and her husband, James Warren, took an active role in protests against the British. The Warren home was a meeting place for revolutionaries, including John Adams, who would be elected president. In 1805, Mercy Warren published a three-volume history of the Revolution.

western frontier—western border; in 1765 it was the Ohio River Valley.

wetlands—low-lying areas along coasts and rivers that are flooded for all or part of the year.

Williamsburg—capital of colonial Virginia.

Wilson, James—(1742–1798) 44-year-old lawyer and Constitutional Convention delegate from Pennsylvania.

winter quarters—place where the army stayed during the winter months, when fighting stopped.

Yorktown—town on Chesapeake Bay, in southeastern Virginia, site of the last major battle of the American Revolution.

Acknowledgements

10, 14, 16 Courtesy of the Library of Congress.
19 © Colonial Williamsburg Foundation.
25 © The Granger Collection.
31, 37, 41 Courtesy of the Library of Congress.
43 © Philadelphia Museum of Art: Bequest of Mrs. Esther B. Wistar to the Historical Society of Pennsylvania in 1900 and acquired by Philadelphia Museum of Art.
44 Courtesy Scott, Foresman and Company.
47, 56, 59, 64, 66, 70, 75, 77, 83, 89, 95, 97, 99, 106, 111, 113, 118, 125, 134 Courtesy of the Library of Congress.

136 © National Museum of American History, Smithsonian Institution.
141, 145, 149 Courtesy of the Library of Congress.
163 © Office of the Architects of the Capitol, U.S. Capitol Historical Society.
162, 165, 171, 173, 178, 183, 184, 193 Courtesy of the Library of Congress.
189, 191 © Smithsonian Institution.